"This is a truly wise, remarkable book! Comprehensive in scope, beautifully written, compellingly illustrated, Cantrell and Lucas illuminate the mind, heart, and soul of high-performing leadership. Wondering whether it's worth buying and reading and applying? Just study the inspiring chapter outline and listen to your conscience for your answer."

Dr. Stephen R. Covey
AUTHOR
The 7 Habits of Highly Effective People
The 8th Habit: From Effectiveness to Greatness

"Clearly, an ethics-free focus on performance is a superb way to destroy performance. . . . But what is perhaps not as obvious is the wealth and good that can come from closely connecting these two powerful concepts—ethics and performance.

In this wonderful book, Wes Cantrell and Jim Lucas show us what this connection looks like, and how it can be put to work to build prosperous organizations and careers.

You should find the style of this book appealing. It is a very personal case study encased in outstanding teaching. The focus is on the career of Wes Cantrell, an excellent leader and CEO who lived the precepts of this book in a forty-six-year career with Lanier.

The teaching comes from Jim Lucas, an internationally recognized authority on leadership and organizational life. . . . You can take what he says to the bank—both figuratively and literally.

High-Performance Ethics is a rare commodity, a book with a truly unique and provocative message that can actually make a difference in the way we act and the results we get today. Its message is as important as any you will hear now or in the years to come."

Steve Forbes
PRESIDENT & CEO, FORBES, INC.
Editor-in-chief, Forbes magazine

"In an ever-changing society and business landscape, we need something solid and real to hang onto. Something that tells us how to do right, something that tells us how to do well.

High-Performance Ethics points the way to that 'something'. . . . This book is based on principles that are thousands of years old, illustrated with examples as current and cutting-edge as today's news.

You will do well to take the message you've received in *High-Performance Ethics* and apply it to your life and career."

Zig Ziglar
AUTHOR AND MOTIVATIONAL TEACHER
Founder, Ziglar

"What a great book. Every young man and woman entering the marketplace would do well to internalize these principles. Every seasoned business veteran will enjoy the story. The section on Life Balance vs. Whole-Life Symmetry is worth the price of the book."

Andy Stanley
PASTOR
North Point Community Church

"*High-Performance Ethics* is a must-read book authored by two people who have lived these principles in the rough and tumble world of corporate America. Wes Cantrell and Jim Lucas have done a masterful job of clearly and practically communicating what it means to be a person of integrity in the marketplace. Read it and you won't be the same."

Howard Dayton
CEO
Compass–Finances God's Way

"Finally, a book that ties high performance and ethics together. You don't have to trade one for the other—you need both, working together, to create the healthiest, most productive work environment possible. Cantrell and Lucas show you how. Don't miss this book if you care about developing your own high-performance, highly ethical skills."

Michael Kroth
AUTHOR AND COAUTHOR
The Manager as Motivator and Transforming Work

"My personal experience of working in the financial world, over the last forty years, is that those who have succeeded in business or who have succeeded personally have, either knowingly or unknowingly, applied biblical wisdom to their decision making. Wes Cantrell is a man who has experience at the very senior level in corporate America. I have known Wes for almost thirty years and have observed that his consistent, growing faith allowed him to perform as a CEO with almost unparalleled success. He ran a huge company always relying upon biblical wisdom in his decision making. He has added his illustrative stories to the rare wisdom that Jim Lucas offers as he unwraps ten enduring principles for today's corporate leaders. Jim draws from a wealth of experience having consulted with teams and leaders across multiple industries for more than two decades. It is a privilege to be able to endorse this book."

Ron Blue
PRESIDENT
Christian Financial Professionals Network

"In *High-Performance Ethics*, Wes shares key insights from his business experiences that were built on a foundation of ethics. He shows how he learned the way of doing well by doing right, and how he learned to trust his business to the Lord when he was on the brink of total failure. This book is a breath of fresh air when corporate giants are crumbling all around us. Wes is a great model, and this book is a must-read for leaders of all ages."

Bobby Mitchell
CHAIRMAN
Fellowship of Companies for Christ International, Franklin Covey

"Cantrell and Lucas remind us that high-performance leadership is ethical, and ethical leadership produces high-performance organizations. This is an *outstanding* book!"

Adam Hamilton
SENIOR PASTOR
The United Methodist Church of the Resurrection

"To know Wes Cantrell is to understand what drives his passion to do what is right. *High-Performance Ethics* presents some great stories that prove biblical principles are highly effective in the workplace, and offers great insight on how we can actually model good behavior. If we're going to talk the talk, we must walk the walk."

S. Truett Cathy
FOUNDER AND CEO
Chick-fil-A

"Business ethics can no longer operate at the margins of organizational life. It must be at the cutting edge of what all organizations care about today. *High-Performance Ethics* by Cantrell and Lucas vividly illustrates how to achieve enduring success through ethics. Indeed, if we are to achieve corporate excellence, the ten ethical values discussed in this book must become embedded in all aspects of our personal and organizational lives."

Phil Lewis
Dean, College of Professional Studies
Oklahoma Christian University

"The writers have laid out biblical principles that when they are embraced will bring blessing to your life. Reading this book will challenge you to study and apply these principles everyday, both in your personal life as well as in business."

David Green
CEO
Hobby Lobby Stores

"Wes Cantrell and James Lucas have written a really good book. It is full of truth and wisdom, liberally seasoned with real-life examples and anecdotes of how to apply the principles it advocates. Scripturally-based and field tested, this book will have a long and valued shelf life, and I expect to use it as a reference point myself."

Dennis Peacocke
President
Strategic Christian Services

"I have found through the years that principles are timeless truths that can be applied to every generation. You will find principles in this book that will not only build your business, but will also build your life. It has been said that you do not have to remember what you said if you tell the truth. This book tells the truth. This truth will change its readers."

Johnny Hunt
Pastor, First Baptist Church of Woodstock
Former President of the Southern Baptist Convention

High-Performance
ETHICS

*10 Timeless Principles for
Next-Generation Leadership*

WES CANTRELL
JAMES R. LUCAS

TYNDALE HOUSE PUBLISHERS, INC.
CAROL STREAM, ILLINOIS

Visit Tyndale online at www.tyndale.com.

Visit the book's Web site at www.highperformanceethics.com. The site includes a powerful assessment you can take.

TYNDALE and Tyndale's quill logo are registered trademarks of Tyndale House Publishers, Inc.

High-Performance Ethics: 10 Timeless Principles for Next-Generation Leadership

Designed by Erik Peterson

Library of Congress Cataloging-in-Publication Data

High-performance ethics : 10 timeless principles for next-generation leadership / Wes Cantrell and James R. Lucas.
  p. cm.
  Includes bibliographical references (p.   ).
  ISBN 978-1-4143-0340-6 (hc)
  1. Conduct of life. 2. Ethics. 3. Success. I. Lucas, J. R. (James Raymond), date. II. Title.
BJ1581.2.C252 2007
170′.44—dc22   2006035034

ISBN 978-1-4143-6534-3 (sc)

Printed in the United States of America

17 16 15 14 13 12 11
 7   6   5   4   3   2   1

DEDICATION

To Bernadine, my loyal wife of fifty years, a person who reminded me in word and deed of the principles of high-performance ethics each time the going got rough, an encourager who believed in me and boosted my confidence when it seemed my world was coming apart, a rock of our Christian faith whom I credit for the success of our family.

In the early 1990s, *Fortune* ran a cover story about "the trophy wife," an attractive, professional second wife who would underscore the success of a CEO and give him more impact, particularly at social events. Bernadine and I had dinner with some *Fortune* executives one evening and she asked them, "Why don't you run an article about the CEOs who are true to their wives?" Their answer: "It wouldn't sell. But it's obvious that Wes married a trophy wife the first time."

Bernadine is the light of my life and I'm still in love with her after fifty years. She is indeed a "trophy wife."

— WES CANTRELL

This book is dedicated to everyone who has tried to do well and do right, and to do well by doing right—and to Peter Drucker, Kermit Gallagher, Robert Townsend, and N. T. Veatch, who showed me how.

— JAMES R. LUCAS

CONTENTS

WANT TO KNOW THE 21ST CENTURY PATH TO SUCCESS?

|||||||||||||||||||||||||||||||||||||||||||||||||||||||||||||||||||||||||||||||||||||||||||||||||||||||||||||||||||||||||||||||||||||||||||||||||||||||||||||||||||||||||||||||||

THERE IS A BETTER way to do business. And this better way—the ethical way—will lead to amazing results: highly committed employees and customers, financial gains, and strong, healthy organizations.

Wes Cantrell, a highly respected and well-known business executive, knows the importance of strong values. In *High-Performance Ethics*, he teams up with Jim Lucas, an internationally recognized leadership consultant, to reveal a truly surprising secret: The road of principle is also the road to higher performance and richer results.

Using ten timeless principles for leadership, richly illustrated with examples from Wes's nearly fifty-year career with Lanier Worldwide, Inc., and ideas from Jim's cutting-edge leadership firm, the authors demonstrate that in order for one to be optimally successful in the marketplace, performance and ethics must go hand in hand. This "leadership book with a twist" offers you practical ways to integrate these two closely connected concepts into your own day-to-day practices—and as you do so, you'll discover a better way to think and live.

FOREWORD

THIS BOOK COULDN'T be more timely. Corporate scandals still reverberate, the latest round concerning the "backdating" of stock options. Before these, there were mutual fund trading abuses and before these, Enron, WorldCom, Adelphi, and others. As we look over the business terrain of the past decade, the disasters that await us if we disconnect ethics from performance are obvious. Clearly, an ethics-free focus on performance is a superb way to destroy performance. The only thing it secures is a strong shot at jail time.

But what is perhaps not as obvious is the wealth and good that can come from closely connecting these two powerful concepts—ethics and performance.

In this wonderful book, Wes Cantrell and Jim Lucas show us what this connection looks like and how it can be put to work to build prosperous organizations and careers.

They bring "ethics" down from a lofty-sounding position in the clouds and make them real principles that real leaders can use to get real results. All too often, ethics are too amorphous or fuzzy or impractical to make any difference "on the ground." Sometimes they don't even make sense. But here we see ethics at work in building businesses, making decisions, dealing with people, developing relationships, and enhancing careers. There's nothing obscure or unhelpful in what Wes and Jim have to say.

And they put the idea of performance in context. They help us realize that genuine success over a long period of time can't be accomplished by building on ethical sands. Make no mistake, they are believers in healthy, strong ambitions and outstanding results. Their message isn't "Be good and still try to do well," but rather, "Be good and you will do well." Push ethics from the backseat to the driver's seat, and your business vehicle will roar ahead.

You should find the style of this book appealing. It is a very personal case study encased in outstanding teaching. The focus is on the career of Wes Cantrell, an excellent leader and CEO who lived the precepts of this book in a forty-six-year career with Lanier. I've known Wes for many years, and I can tell you that what he says is genuine, on point, and proven by a great track record on both ethics and performance.

The teaching comes from Jim Lucas, an internationally recognized authority on leadership and organizational life. Jim has addressed these and other topics in four previous books, in keynote addresses, and in countless other presentations. He has a thriving consulting practice. He's seen what works—and what doesn't work—in numerous organizations and careers. You can take what he says to the bank, both figuratively and literally.

High-Performance Ethics is a rare commodity, a book with a truly unique and provocative message that can actually make a difference in the way we act and the results we get today. Its message is as important as any you will hear now or in the years to come.

—Steve Forbes
President and CEO of Forbes, Inc.
Editor-in-chief of *Forbes* magazine

ETHICS & HIGH PERFORMANCE

The Remarkable Connection

IN A FRIGHTENINGLY real sense, no organization is far from the edge of meltdown: ethical collapse followed by financial ruin.

One of the great companies of the last century was Merck, a pharmaceutical giant whose leaders made their values the centerpiece of the company's existence. They worried first about research and improving people's lives and health, and then about sales and growth. The company created drugs that would never be profitable, and then gave them away. Merck had done *right*, and it had done *well* by doing right.

And then came Vioxx—one drug in Merck's long and moral corporate history—and, without the guidance of *high-performance ethics*,[1] this giant stumbled. The company missed the mark at one end, by not being transparent when studies revealed potential negative effects of the drug. Then it missed it at the other end, by going beyond simple warnings to pulling the drug from the market and opening itself up to every lawyer in the Western world (the whole world, perhaps).

The first approach failed because it kept important information from a very small percentage of patients who could be *hurt* by the drug. The second approach failed because it kept an important drug from a very large percentage of patients who could be *helped* by it.

1

In the language of an ancient Hebrew proverb, Merck swung from being not righteous enough to being overly righteous. In that proverb, the penalty for acting without enough righteousness is to "die before your time," and the penalty for acting overly righteous is to "destroy yourself."[2] Merck may survive this self-inflicted disaster, but even so, it will have tarnished its reputation as the ethical gold standard for investors, employees, and other stakeholders.

There are debacles like Enron, where the organization is sick at the core, and where every nonconscience, non-sense step moves it further from high-performance ethics. And then there are tragedies like Merck, where the organization is largely decent but tries to compensate for one guilty and destructive action with another.

The potential costs are too high—and the potential competitive advantages too great—to miss the power of high-performance ethics.

Is There Really an Ethics-Performance Connection?

Did ethical breakdown have anything to do with Merck's performance meltdown? Well, yes. It had *everything* to do with it. Character really is destiny, for organizations as well as individuals.[3]

So let's get right down to it: What can something as intangible and hard to measure as ethics possibly have to do with something as "real-world" and relentlessly measured as high performance?

Sure, ethics might make you a kinder, gentler leader, but how can they make any difference in the performance and results you're expected to deliver in a hard-boiled world?

All too often, ethics and performance are viewed as unrelated concepts, like cell phones and solitude, or television and reflection. Of course, most would agree (at least superficially) that we should be decent and caring, but when we cut through the gaudy oratory of annual reports and press releases and get down to reality, many organizations consider ethics an expendable luxury.

So What Are Ethics, and Where Do They Come From?

Part of the reason we don't always value ethics is that we aren't sure what they are and where they originate.

Are ethics something we can just make up? And if so, who gets to decide what they are? Some view ethics as simple platitudes, like the bromides children learn today in school (for example, "We are respectful . . . tolerant . . . nice"). Others consider ethics merely as moral fine points for academic debate, disputes best dropped when we move on to the real-world business of building successful organizations. Still others see ethics as the leftovers of a centuries-old human experiment in living together in society, or maybe an otherworldly collection of religious teachings. Whatever definition we choose from this list, we seem to be left with a chintzy version of ethics, a meager echo of past philosophies.

One writer on this subject recently proclaimed, "Most of us know right from wrong," so that the "essential challenge of moral intelligence is not knowing right from wrong, but doing versus knowing."[4] But in a world where phrases like "your truth and my truth" are the norm and disasters like the Enron scandal are commonplace, the writer's claim that most people know right from wrong seems highly questionable. In fact, this expert rattles his own argument: "We don't always agree on what is right," he admits. He goes on to argue that "no one philosophy is 'better' than another,"[5] and concludes that "within each of us are the values and basis for our moral compass."[6]

The problems with this argument are legion. Most important, many people actually *don't* know right from wrong. They just don't get it, or even want to get it. Many others often feel that ethically, they're in a dark room with a very small candle and too many shadows. Comparing various operating philosophies isn't going to make the distinction between right and wrong any clearer. Without a source of truth to rely on, without a standard to measure these philosophies against, we're all just making things up as we go.

Instead of staking our lives and organizations on the solid principles that can ultimately produce high performance,[7] we're instead likely to mold our "ethics" to fit our ambitions, goals, and desires.

Pathetic "Ethics" and the Forces That Devastate Them

These lily-livered, self-made, self-interested, cardboard "ethics" are unlikely to survive three highly detrimental and interrelated forces.

The first force is (and has been from time immemorial) a basic human desire to look out for ourselves, all too often without regard for others—and not infrequently at their expense. Humans have an undeniable orientation toward selfishness and greed. We focus on getting what we want when we want it.

The second force arrayed against puny ethics is society's ongoing attempt to remove bedrock values from public and private life—to reduce ethics to a lowest common denominator so that they offend no one. Unfortunately, the loss of these values has the potential to harm a lot more than our organizations or families. When people lose any sense of the connection between freedom and prosperity on the one hand, and the underlying values that produce them on the other, it is only a matter of time before the freedom and prosperity deteriorate and then finally evaporate.

The third force that erodes flimsy ethics is the idea that people are merely the physical products of a long, random, mindless process, rather than complex spiritual beings who can make choices (and who should therefore be responsible for their actions). Setting aside the current debate about overarching biological processes, it's hard to imagine how a view of human life based only on survival of the fittest (surely not the most honorable ideal) leaves any room for ethics. Such a view demands that might *makes* right. Where in this worldview is the call to pass up an opportunity because it is marginally wrong, even if it will increase our market share? Why stand up for a principle when there appears to be no material advantage? People who embrace this brutal outlook on life eventually come to see that they have no compelling reason to care for the most vulnerable people in an organization or society, or even for the earth and its resources. If a species becomes extinct or a careless organization destroys an ecosystem or twenty-five thousand careers, why should they mourn? Isn't this just the way the world works?

The Durability and Triumph of Solid Ethics

In this book we respectfully suggest that there is a better way to think and live. And this better way—the ethical way—happens to lead to an outcome so counterintuitive that even sharp, highly placed leaders frequently miss the connection.

The road of principle *is* the road to higher performance and richer results.*

> Many people have asked me just when it was that I decided I was going to become president of Lanier. Was it when I was first moved up into management as a sales/branch manager back in 1959? Or maybe when I became the district manager in 1962? Perhaps in 1972, when I became national sales manager? The answer to that question surprises most everyone who asks. You see, I never actually decided that being president was my overriding objective. I believed that the most important thing I could do for the company and for myself was to assure success in my present position and not to focus on some personal dream for the future to the neglect of current realities. There were many executives I knew who wanted their next promotion so much that they were willing to do almost anything. In many cases, exaggerated results that looked good on the surface turned out not to be so good once time had passed and audit information had become available.

* *Throughout the book, the vertical line denotes Wes Cantrell recounting highlights from his career.*

My consistent message to the field was, "Build a strong team in your present position, just as though you were going to be in that same job for the rest of your life." I believe that is the way to build a successful career and a great company.

That's not to say that I hadn't thought about the fact that someday Lanier would need a president. My boss, Gene Milner, was chairman, and the company would be going public in 1977. By that point, I was doing the job of the chief operating officer and I knew that I could possibly be a candidate for president. Although I wanted the job, I chose not to focus on it. I knew it wouldn't be healthy for the company—or for me personally—to concentrate on anything but doing my current job well.

A Lanier family member who worked under my direction was the most likely candidate to be president. I had always heard that blood is thicker than water, and I thought in the final analysis he would probably be the family's choice.

Doing the right thing rather than trying to claw our way to the top is a much better way to live. But it also positions us to be successful where we are, to earn trust, and to be available and prepared when new opportunities present themselves. Texas Instruments declares that "We view our reputation . . . as important an asset as the high technologies that we develop and bring to our marketplace."[8] As Stephen Covey notes: "The only way to acquire moral authority is through your character and contribution, to live in such a way as to merit the confidence and trust of other people. Moral authority is especially important to business. This is because in order to reduce costs, increase production, and nurture a culture of innovation—all of which are important criteria in today's global economy—you've got to have high trust among your workers and partners."[9]

Ethics are derived from bedrock spiritual principles that people can know and understand. Of course, character must be developed and disciplined if we want the integrity to move beyond lip service and actually live our ethics. Great leaders live the principle, "Whatever your hand finds to do, do it with all your might."[10] Even while watching others push for success directly, these leaders stick to their principles and mentor their teams to do the same. They stay focused and work hard, always keeping their ethics in the foreground.

The truly surprising fact—something people frequently miss when they calculate an assumed trade-off between principle and performance—is that *ethical leadership creates high performance*. By doing *good*, we can do *well*.

> In mid-summer 1977, Gene asked me to set up a meeting honoring Sartain Lanier. We had just finished a good year and I had a special plaque prepared for Mr. Lanier relating to our results. I planned to make the presentation during our meeting at the Terrace Garden Inn in Buckhead, the high-rent district of Atlanta. All the top executives arrived and we had a nice lunch.
>
> Just as we were preparing to start the ceremony, my wife walked in. I knew then that something unexpected was happening, something that involved me. The element of surprise made it even more special.
>
> Gene Milner stood up and began to talk. He briefly reviewed my twenty-two-year career with Lanier, emphasizing my dedication and hard work. Then he announced that I had been elected president of Lanier by the Board of Directors. I was elated; I could hardly believe my ears. Gene presented a letter to me, which I have framed and hanging on my office wall, which reads as follows:
>
> *Dear Wes:*
> *I consider it a great privilege to inform you that the Board of Directors has elected you President of Lanier Business Products. This honor and position with this company is deserved by your*

> *tremendous and effective performance over the last twenty-*
> *one plus years. Your integrity, ability, loyalty, and exceedingly*
> *hard work have made this a most deserved promotion.*
> *Much appreciation for your past performance and many*
> *congratulations on your promotion.*
> *Cordially,*
> *Gene W. Milner*
> *Chairman of the Board*

An unexpressed personal dream came true, and since the company was going public, the timing could not have been better! We were off on the most exciting journey anyone could imagine, and I had the job that down deep in my heart I had always wanted—but had not sought.

Too often, ethics and high performance are regarded as two distinct and largely unrelated subjects. But there is a deep and intimate connection between them. Ethics that draw on the best in leaders, people, teams, and organizations can provide a truly sustainable competitive advantage over organizations that lack a strong commitment to values. Citing the Dow Jones Sustainability Group Index, one study noted that "companies using 'triple bottom line' measures of economic, environmental, and ethical sustainability outperform other companies on the stock market."[11] Another reported, "approximately 46 percent of EBIT (earnings before interest and taxes) is explained by the variable of corporate culture, or cultural 'buy-in,'"[12] at least a portion of which includes ethical commitment.

It is difficult (if not impossible) to sustain high performance in a values vacuum—as Enron proved when the company made it into the Fortune 10 and was named the "most creative company in America," right before an integrity outage led to its total collapse.[13] The problem is that *any* organization could grow up to be like Enron. Innovation in the business model can easily devolve into innovation in ethics, truth telling, and accounting.

"A company is doomed to mediocrity," said Howard Schultz, founder and CEO of Starbucks, "unless it has passionate staff who believe in its values and its message. . . . If you don't have passionate people believing in the values of your company, your message will be diluted and mediocrity will set in."[14] And they can't believe in the values if you don't have them.

Principles Need More than a Friendly Nod

In order to reap the benefits of high performance, we have to cultivate our principles over time, building them into our characters and organizations, training our consciences to know right from wrong, and disciplining ourselves to choose right—even when those right choices cost something in the short run. Long-term success is more than focus and hard work and talent and commitment. It's also integrity that stands out so clearly that others can't help but see it.

We never really know when and how our integrity will be judged, which is one reason that leaders simply can't afford to switch their principles off or on in response to the needs of the moment. Situational ethics are no ethics at all.

> For some time, I pondered how this promotion had happened. My mind drifted back to the late 1950s, shortly after I'd started with Lanier. I was a salesman in Augusta, Georgia, at the time and I was in Atlanta for a meeting. Gene called me aside and suggested we have a private luncheon, away from our group. I knew this meant that he had something he wanted to discuss with me, something important.
>
> As we were having lunch, Gene said, "I've heard that you will not even have so much as a social drink. Is that true?" I confirmed his suspicions, and he became direct and strong. He wasn't exactly angry, but he glared at me as he told me,

"You'll never make it big in Lanier unless you start drinking."
He added that he would be insulted if I invited him over to
my home for dinner and didn't offer him a drink.

I thought carefully about the commitment I had made as a
young man. In a Sunday school class, I had made a promise to
God and myself that I would not use tobacco or drink alcoholic
beverages. I was aware that many Christians don't believe these
habits to be wrong, but I was convinced that these habits were
not for me. And now, the real question was whether I would
honor my commitment. I remembered my promise and decided
that I must keep it.

Carefully considering my choice of words and mustering
my courage, I replied, "I guess I'll have to be your best salesman in Augusta for the rest of my life." Gene looked at me for a
long time, and then we returned to our meeting with no further
discussion. To say this was uncomfortable would be a grand
understatement.

Was this the same man who would one day announce my
promotion to the position of president? The same man who
said I "would never make it big"? Wasn't the job of president
"making it big"?

Whatever Gene's intent, I knew that the proposition he
presented was a test. The one agenda item for the lunch was
drinking. The man who ultimately controlled my career was
testing me—would I compromise?

I now believe that if I had compromised, Gene would have
lost confidence in me. He was checking to see if I would stick to
my guns—even when it might cost me something that was very
important to me. He had little respect for those who wouldn't
stand up to him.

Little did I know how important that luncheon discussion
was and how a compromise then would have certainly cost me
the opportunity to "make it big" in the years to come. In that

moment, the first stepping-stones were laid that would provide a path to future changes at Lanier, changes about which I could only dream early in my career.

For Gene Milner, the real issue was Wes's character, not whether or not he would take a drink. In fact, Gene was actually hoping Wes would stick to a position with which Gene himself did not even agree. When we take a stand on principles, people will always be watching to see if we stick by those principles under pressure. Their disagreement with our principles might be secondary to their judgment of our character. Will we hold to our commitments despite the fierce disapproval of others—especially people who count?

Sticking by Principles Has a Cost, Not Just a Payoff

To be sure, there are others who have suggested that we can do well by doing right. The bookstores are filled with business leadership books that try to incentivize readers to do right by showing that there is a payoff. Some of their advice is so basic as to be useless in the real world of politics, economics, culture, business, or relationships.[15] Some of it derives from complex philosophical systems that lack business relevance. But the fundamental problem with many of these teachings is that they miss the fact that the payoff from good principles is a lot like happiness: It is a by-product of living a life of value and integrity, not something we can go after directly.

In the long run, ethical leadership builds high performance and unmatched results, a reputation for trustworthiness, and enduring success. In the short run, however, we may feel that we're missing an opportunity or paying a steep price for holding to our principles.

Samuel Goldwyn of MGM fame once said, "I don't want any 'yes' men. . . . I want people to tell me the truth, even if it costs them their jobs." How do principles help when we are faced with a situation where speaking the truth could cost us our jobs (or clients or customers)? In such a case, sticking up for truth brings risk or even short-term loss.

Even in organizations that have taken the time to identify their core values, those values too often are dropped when the short-term costs seem to outweigh the long-term benefits. But what is the worth of a value like integrity if it doesn't include telling the truth when it costs something? Does having integrity simply mean that we won't overtly lie or steal? Or does integrity include, for example, expressing disagreement rather than pretending to agree in order to earn a few points with someone in power?

Either there is a playbook of fixed principles or there isn't, and if there isn't, then ethics are very fragile indeed, likely to shatter at the first sign of difficulty or personal sacrifice. But ethics based on bedrock principles are clear, actionable, and (if we build our lives and organizations on them) inevitably tied to producing high performance that can be sustained over time.[16]

So What Are High-Performance Ethics?

High-performance ethics (HPE) are a way of life—the way of doing well by doing right. HPE means doing right with the absolute conviction that there will be commensurate (maybe even disproportionately large) rewards—even as we face setbacks and make short-term sacrifices for the sake of principle.

High-performance ethics are practical ideas that have been derived from long-standing core principles. HPE leaders dissect those principles with the goal of applying them to human performance, both individually and collectively.

Before we go much further, it will be helpful to describe what high-performance ethics are *not*. High-performance ethics are different from either high performance or ethics. It is possible to achieve some level of high performance without doing right; indeed, it is possible to achieve it by doing wrong. And it is possible to do right without achieving high performance. Visiting a sick or dying person, consoling a friend, assisting the down-and-out, giving to a charity—all are very good things that often have no direct bearing on professional high performance.

In a sense, high-performance ethics are a fusion of high-performance thinking with ethical thinking. But high-performance ethics constitute something different from either, a marriage of concepts with a combined power greater than their sum.

Two Bad Alternatives to High-Performance Ethics

Of course, there are alternatives to high-performance ethics, albeit *ineffective* alternatives.

Ethics "policies" became the fad of the moment in the late 1980s, and most publicly traded companies have some sort of code of ethics even today. In many cases, however, these ethics statements have made no difference in the way these organizations have operated. Is the purpose of these policies just to foster good public relations? Or are principles and the convictions of corporate leaders truly reflected in those codes? The evidence indicates that in many cases it has just been good (or as it turns out, bad) PR.

Government legislation won't get the job done, either. For some reason, humans have a natural tendency to try to legislate morality. We want to avoid the hard work of building character on enduring principles, of educating for the intangibles, of rewarding on the so-called "soft" issues, of eliminating (quickly) the bad actors even if they are producing, and of finding ways to connect living right and doing well. Instead, we often go for the shortest, the quick fix of rules and regulations—the fix that doesn't fix.

On a national level, massive systems like HIPPA and Sarbanes-Oxley are created in the hope that they will create better performers and better people. Instead, these measures often succeed only in creating new "growth" industries that waste countless hours and resources in public and private companies, destroy the ability to deliver needed services in always-struggling not-for-profits, and inject more senseless bureaucracy into government.

The evidence indicates that confidence in codes of conduct or rules and regulations is probably misplaced—if not illusory. A recent article in *CFO* magazine asked, "Is there any reason to believe that all these codes and classes and scenarios do any good? The evidence is mixed. A recent survey of more than 4,000 employees found that reports of misdeeds had not diminished."[17] The article reported "the same level of wrongdoing [as] reported in a pre-Sarbanes-Oxley survey," and noted that "if employees don't know right from wrong by the time they enter the workforce, no ethics program on the planet will fill the gap."[18]

The problem stems in part from contrasting ethics with performance, instead of combining them. "Remarkably, half of the respondents who said their companies have comprehensive ethics programs also noted that they felt pressure to 'do whatever it takes to meet targets.'"[19] This can go right down to the individual level. "Companies not known for stretching the truth may have their own practices that encourage bad behavior. At the top of the list: performance reviews that focus primarily on quantitative measures . . . employees should not be judged solely on what they do, but also on how they do it."[20] The norm is to separate performance from ethics. HPE leaders create a new norm by merging them.

This isn't an argument against having any laws or rules, and it certainly isn't an argument to ignore the ones that exist. But it is fair to ask hard questions: Can we legislate our way to integrity? Will rules or ethics codes make us better people? Can regulations do what firm principles and character and community cannot? Are all these policies really increasing the level of ethical behavior?

In tackling these issues, we must be wary of delusion. When we fail to build our character and our organizations on enduring spiritual principles, we find that codes and laws seem made to be broken. Laws and rules simply cannot put in what people leave out.

The Real Deal

High-performance ethics have real-world impact on lives and organizations—and on the bottom line. Leaders abandon these principles at their peril, or align with them to their infinite gain. In this book, we will relate these principles to the high-paced, high-stakes world that leaders—that *you*—face right now.

HPE leaders use their wisdom, knowledge, experience, power, energy, attention, confidence, and humility to implement the foundational principles we'll discuss in the chapters that follow. One leader reminds us, "The one thing that doesn't go away in a company is the character and humanity of its leader . . . that person has to be the best listener, the best interpreter, and the most passionate driver of the company's purpose."[21] Organizations consist of much more than what they *do*. They consist of who they *are*.

Legacy seekers must focus on building traits that define an influential character: wisdom (rather than simple knowledge); integrity (being honest with ourselves as well as others); a passion for life, work, and people; enough confidence to know what we're about and enough humility to know that others can help us to be better; and self-control. Rather than asking, "What will people think of this?" the HPE leader asks, "What's the right thing to do?"

They know that you can do well and do right, and do well by doing right. They're willing to take short-term losses because they want to avoid the biggest loss of all—themselves.

Should we run our organizations with a focus on principles or with a focus on performance? *Definitely.*[22] Paradoxically, if we run our organizations with these "better ideas," we create organizations that also deliver sustainable top-tier results. High-performance ethics are not just motivational-speech platitudes and high-sounding moral statements. They are a fabulous set of revealed principles that open the door to unimaginably rich results.

We invite you to learn them, apply them, live them—and prosper.

INTRODUCTION

||||||||||||||||||||||||||||||||||||||||||||||||||||||||||||||||||||||||||||||||||||||||||||||||||||||||||||||||||||||||||||||||||||||||||

FIRST THINGS ONLY

You can be great with the right priorities

THE FIRST PRINCIPLE of high-performance ethics (HPE) targets priorities. It requires us to get the right things in the right order. This principle is a challenge to set our minds on things that matter, rather than on the mundane and fleeting—or even on the things that matter, but not as much.

Plenty of experts have highlighted the vital need to get first things first, to focus on the important (not just the urgent), and to guard time for faith and family. But HPE leaders know that in addition to being obvious, these ideas are merely an entry fee. They're necessary but not sufficient. They don't tell us what's important, or how much time to spend on it once we figure it out.

In business terms, "first things *only*" means taking the time to define what's really important to the life and health of our organizations. If we get this principle right, everything else will fall into place—and if we don't, everything else will fall apart. There are only a few "first things," not a hundred or a thousand, and once we find them we don't take our eyes off them for a second. First things *only* means crafting a worthy vision and mission, agreeing on values, and deciding who we are and what our organizations should exist to do. As we act on this first principle, we begin by helping our people to focus on big things and broadening their vision before we narrow their focus to the business at hand.[1]

Most organizations don't have passion—certainly not at the front lines. It can't be trained. It can't be bought. It can only be released by designing an organization in which people consider it wise to invest their lives and talents. Even competence, as important as it is, can't be developed much if passion and talent are lacking. As we forge a shared vision and mission together with our employees, and define important values and behaviors,[2] we ignite and direct the passion in our organizations.[3] Only first things stir greatness.

Start with a Powerful, Shared Vision and Mission

Leaders have the power to implement this principle at the organizational level, first by bringing everyone into the vision and mission development process, and then by bringing competent people who share the vision and values into the organization. Each individual must also act on this principle—choosing to invest passionately in the vision and mission, upholding the organization's values, practicing the behaviors that exhibit those values, and working with competence. Get the organizational and individual elements of this principle into alignment, and the organization will have a powerful culture that produces world-class results.*

> As a leader at Lanier, Gene Milner was a man who had a plan and knew where he was going. In 1965, I was visiting my parents in Georgia. Gene called and suggested we have dinner while I was in town.
>
> I met him at the old Marriott on Courtland Street in downtown Atlanta, and over dinner, Gene decided to tell me about his plans. Ten years into my career, I was now the district manager in Baton Rouge and had begun to do quite well. That night,

---

* Throughout the book, the vertical line denotes Wes Cantrell recounting highlights from his career.

Check Out Receipt

Post Road Library

www.forsythpl.org

Thursday, July 20, 2017 5:38:56 PM
60359

Item: 1002520307
Title: High-performance ethics : 10 timeless principles for next-generation leadership
Material: Paperback Book
Due: 08/03/2017

Item: 1002531138
Title: Change your life with NLP : the powerful way to make your whole life better with neuro-linguisitic programming
Material: Paperback Book
Due: 08/03/2017

Total items: 2

Please note: Accounts with fines or other fees totaling $10.00 or more are sent to Debt Collection.

Register for Summer Reading Fun through July 31 and join in on the fun!

Gene shared with me his dream for the future of the company. Whether or not he shared his thoughts with anyone else is unknown to me. But he told me in no uncertain terms that we would buy our major suppliers. They were weak and we understood distribution, which was more important in our industry. (When I asked about 3M, Gene said we would only buy their copier business, not the entire company, which was certainly more reasonable!) First, we would become a national company, then international business would come later. Gene had big plans, and he made me privy to his thoughts that evening. Needless to say, these were really big plans for a company whose total revenue was only about $12 million at that time.

I bought the vision hook, line, and sinker! My thoughts rushing to this planned success, I was extremely excited as I returned to Baton Rouge. In my enthusiasm, I talked to my fellow employees about our future, and they caught my excitement and enthusiasm. At our Christmas party that year, they gave me a present, which I still have on the wall of my office. It's a walnut-inlayed orange-peel map of the world. When they gave it to me, they said, "This is your territory." Evidently, they shared the vision.

Years later, every single thing Gene talked about over dinner in 1965 actually happened, clearly demonstrating the power of vision. We bought all of our suppliers and became a national company. Later, with the acquisition of 3M's copier/fax business, we became an international player. All of these acquisitions made it possible for us eventually to become a $1.5 billion company.

HPE leaders believe in the power of vision and are willing to share that vision with people "down the line." When our people catch the vision, they will fuel their teams and the organization to achieve it.

There truly is power in shared vision and mission, and in answering the big questions first: Where are we going (vision), and what will we do to get there (mission)? Vision means purpose: Why do we exist? What *is* our long-term future? And mission is a set of clearly defined "critical success factors": What are the things we must do, and do well, if we intend to achieve our vision?

Simply having a vision and mission and passing out copies will not be enough. Working with countless leaders and organizations, I have seen how values are lost and opportunities are missed when these priorities are considered to be in the domain only of brilliant, charismatic people at the top. The power of vision and mission is multiplied many times over when our people participate in developing and enhancing that vision and mission with us.

When we move from informing to involving people in the process of creating the vision and mission, everyone begins to think about first things only, opening our organizations up to the potential for unimagined success. Unfortunately, many leaders are reticent to include their people in discussions of first things, and thus forfeit the success that could be theirs.

> The night he shared his vision with me had been an exception for Gene. He was not naturally one to discuss goals, objectives, and strategy. He had always been inclined to tell people what to do, but not why. Some of his orders were hard to understand because of this style. He certainly never put anything in writing about vision, mission, or long-term goals. I believe he didn't want to be pinned down. In addition, he tested others' loyalty by this question: "Will they follow my directions regardless of what I ask?"
>
> In the late 1970s Lanier's first vision and mission statement was put together. As president of Lanier, I personally did most of the work heading the project to develop it. When I showed it to Gene, he said, "Don't waste your time on stuff like this." But I remembered how powerful our discussion of vision had been for

me years earlier, and I wanted to include our people in a similar discussion about Lanier's vision. We began using this vision and mission statement in high-level presentations. One of the most notable was the presentation to the Harris Corporation when we sold the company to them in 1983. They were particularly impressed with our vision and plans. Personally, I felt a great sense of satisfaction knowing that I had a strategic part in laying the groundwork for the company's future.

What's the use of having a vision if no one shares it? Few people want to be sold on someone else's vision, and the ones who do are most likely to be passive followers rather than active participants. HPE leaders seek robust discussion, debate, disagreement, and a general donnybrook to make the vision and mission the best they can be, and to ensure the highest level of investment in them. One person's vision isn't enough for all of the excellent people who will be needed and expected to fulfill it.

A Powerful Vision Demands Powerful Values

With a shared vision and mission established, we can begin to identify the values and behaviors that will characterize our organizations as we journey toward the goal. How will we act and interact so that we can actually achieve our vision and mission?

Hicks Lanier, one of Lanier's founders and its CEO, respected my values, and he let me know it in his unusual fashion. Once when we were discussing the need for a traveling service representative, he recommended someone who was competent as well as quite open about his Christian beliefs.

"Put Paul in that job," Hicks told me. "He doesn't drink or chase women, so he won't get in trouble." Paul didn't take the job because he wanted to be home with his family, but he would have been a great choice. There were several traveling reps who did get in trouble. The temptations on the road are many, and only someone with strong values can survive. That's what Hicks was looking for.

People know our values, whether or not we advertise them. The longer they work with us, the more people will see and feel the organization's real character. As with vision and mission, integrating values and behaviors into the organization's culture requires that we define them through an inclusive process.

This process needs to include robust discussion of what the values are and how they should look in practice. If we don't define the behaviors that exhibit our values, people will attach their own meanings to them. The net result will be that we *have* no shared values. Lists of single-word values are so generic that they are almost meaningless. For example, *loyalty* can be defined either as "don't rock the boat," or (better) as "love the boat so much you'll rock it if there's a problem."

We Need People of Character and Competence

If we can agree upon why we're here, what our critical success factors for achieving our vision are, what we value, and how we will act and interact, we're ready to consider the next important priority of organizational life: bringing in people who have character and competence. Ultimately, it doesn't matter what we believe if we don't also deliver results. "Show me your faith without deeds," noted an ancient writer, "and I will show you my faith by what I do."[4]

We must select leaders, mentors, partners, and employees who have proven character and competence. These men and women will provide good counsel out of their experience, as well as through knowing us and understanding what we expect. As Wes likes to point out, if you're hiring a pilot, you first need to know whether he can fly the plane. Character is a wonderful and needed attribute, but if he doesn't know how to pilot the plane, there's no need to interview him. Of course if he doesn't have character, he might make poor safety decisions like getting drunk before flying.

I learned the hard way that we must carefully investigate both character *and* competence. People must have both attributes—character and competence—if we are to build a group of wise partners and counselors. The same thing is true in the hiring and promotion decisions leaders make every day.

Few leaders know how to identify either character or competence. Character is "a person's characteristics, the mental and moral features that distinguish that person from others, a person's moral strength and quality of reputation."[5] In the world of business, character is what makes you *you*, what makes you smart or dull, good or bad, strong or weak, and delightful or obnoxious to others. It's the most important feature of every person,[6] but very few leaders put forth genuine effort to look for it. In a recent survey, 75 percent of employers said they don't screen effectively for the job applicant's moral character.[7] Is character hard to discern, and even harder to measure? Of course. But this is no reason not to try. Without a sense of someone's character, we can only hope that he or she will be a fine employee, and plan to correct any deficiencies on an ad hoc basis. This is most assuredly not a formula for building high-quality, unbreakable performance.

Competence means more than just knowing how to "do stuff." Competence means knowing how to do something well, how to focus on what's most important, how best to add value, how to perform a task fearlessly, and how to do it with confidence and ease and comfort. It includes setting, meeting, and exceeding high standards of performance and quality, standards that are ever evolving and rising, and being able to do this because *we're* ever evolving and rising.

Rather than focusing on character and competence, leaders often tend to ask the wrong questions because they feel hamstrung by legal technicalities. Many want to shorten the process because they just need to "get someone on board." But this results in far too many slots being filled with people who have neither the character nor the competence that we need.[8] Some leaders fail to do right because they have too few people of character, and they fail to do well because they have too few people of competence.

Organizations often fail to prioritize character and competence because "human resources" departments often fail to understand that their first priority is *people*. They too easily put legal issues, policy formation and enforcement, and detailed transactions at the top of their list. If they spent more time working the human side of their organizations, they would probably need to spend much less time on legalities (committed people generally don't sue) and policies (committed people generally want to do the right thing). Putting first things *only* means building values-driven—rather than compliance-driven—organizations.

If we have the right people—people of character and competence, believers and winners—who have a mutual, passionate commitment to shared vision, mission, values, and behaviors,[9] we can relax our focus on the tools of control and management. Too many leaders spend their energy focusing on a small percentage of bad apples rather than on the bushels of good ones.

I felt that Hicks Lanier and Gene Milner were both control freaks, but I concluded that I did not have to pattern my management style after theirs. At the same time, I learned a lot from both of these men. We can always learn from others—the things we do not want to emulate as well as those qualities that we do want in our lives. They were attempting to establish their own superiority; maybe they felt that they needed to do so in order to maintain control.

I began to see that the pathway to outstanding leadership requires us to build relationships with our people based on trust and integrity. My desire as a leader was to serve my team members just as we did our customers. I wanted them to be motivated with a vision for a bright future, so I tried to paint a picture of the future and then put them into that picture. I saw that it was important to make sure that they had the resources to do their job, and I tried to offer helpful suggestions rather than constant criticism. After all, if I found it necessary to criticize a person constantly, I probably had the wrong person.

Terms like "chain of command" and "direct reports" are the language of control and subservience. As I've told thousands of leaders, if the first thought that enters your mind every morning is *I need to manage X*, the second thought should be *I need to fire X*.

No amount of control or criticism can produce passion, commitment, dedication, creativity, or anything else of deep and sustainable value. Life is too short to spend time fixing character defects or trying to conjure up competence out of thin talent.

What if alignment is poor or non-existent? Is it always moral or profitable to try to "fix" things to get alignment? HPE leaders know the answer is "no." Fixing things can be a *huge* distraction and an incredible waste of time. It can lead to a net reduction in performance (by misdirecting us and keeping sub-optimal associates) and a watering-down of ethics (by misspending our time and keeping people tied to what they cannot or will not embrace).

To know if a fix is the right answer, we have to find strong answers to questions like these:

>> Has this person exhibited any interest in, or passion for, who we are and what we're trying to accomplish? Does this person care?
>> Has this person shown initiative in mastering our message? Does this person "get it"?
>> Has this person shown an interest in others, in helping them develop and achieve?
>> Has this person tried to grow the job, rather than just doing the job? Is this person adding real value rather than doing the bare minimum?

1: FIRST THINGS ONLY

» Has this person expressed ideas about how to enhance who we are, rather than simply to reshape us into his or her own image?
» Is this person showing responsibility, embracing accountability, and caring about even the little things, rather than having to be reminded and prodded?
» Does this person stay on point rather than wandering off into side issues or petty actions?

If the answer to all of the above is "yes," then fix. Otherwise, let the person go.

"First Things *Only*" Creates High-Performance Culture

The "first things only" principle is the foundation for building a powerful culture, like the *Kaizen* culture of Japan. This culture puts shared vision, values, behaviors, and competence together at the corporate and individual level to achieve a singularly effective outcome.

> Fear and apprehension gripped my heart as we flew at 35,000 feet above the Pacific Ocean. It was 1983, Lanier had just been acquired by Harris Corporation, and I was on my way to Japan for the first time to meet our colleagues there. Recently the Soviets had shot down a Korean airliner when it strayed off course and passed over Sakhalin Island. We were on the same course to Tokyo and I could visualize what had happened just a few weeks earlier. I began to think about what was ahead.
>
> My friend and colleague Nicky Bolick was with me. Nicky had been to Japan many times, and he was showing me the ropes. We had spent many hours talking about the customs in Japan and business protocol. I had read a few books, but I was apprehensive. I didn't want to appear ungrateful or rigid. As president of Lanier and Senior V.P. of Harris, I knew our

Japanese colleagues would honor me because respect is part of their culture, but I wanted to build strong relationships with our friends in Japan.

Doing business in Japan requires an understanding of the culture. Unlike the United States, Japan has never been considered a "melting pot." It has a more uniform culture, which is perhaps both a strength and a weakness.

I had learned about the Japanese business customs, like bowing and exchanging business cards by presenting them with both hands. I knew to use *san* after the last name as a proper greeting of honor and respect, and I had practiced eating with chopsticks. In many ways, I was ready for this new adventure, but never could I have imagined all that I was to learn in the next few years.

When we landed at Narita, it took almost an hour to get to our hotel in Tokyo. The time zone is fourteen hours different from U.S. Eastern Standard—that will turn your biological clock upside down! It was nighttime, but I was wide awake. Very little sleep and lots of coffee seemed to be the only way to work effectively while my body slowly adjusted.

The next day, we began our meetings. Under our new arrangement, we would design the appearance and features of our dictation products in Atlanta, and our partners in Japan would do the mechanical and electronic design. We marveled at how quickly the Japanese engineers responded to our suggested changes and how well they worked with our ideas. It was clear to me that something in their culture was very different from what I had experienced in the United States.

When we asked for a new feature or a better price, they would always say, "We'll go study." In almost every case, they came back with good ideas for reducing our costs, and they always gave us the features we needed to preserve and grow our leading share of the U.S. dictation systems market. It was clear that our Japanese partners truly believed in *Kaizen*—"continuous improvement"—and it permeated all that they did.

By 1987, when I became CEO of Harris/3M (a joint venture that combined Lanier's copier business with 3M's worldwide copier and fax business), my trips to Japan mostly involved our copier suppliers. Toshiba, our major supplier for copiers and dictation products, was quick to adopt our customer-based studies for product improvement, and they always involved us in the new product development cycle.

Once during the development of a new copier, the Toshiba executives told me that of the fifty-six ideas we had submitted for improving the product, they had adopted forty-six of them. The *Kaizen* culture made this second nature for them.

There is great value in common ground. When something strong unites people at the core—in this case, the strongly shared Japanese business value of improving the product—it frees them from the waste that comes from battling over everything in turf wars.

While Wes was at Lanier, the company exhibited the power of vision and values—especially a focus on customer service—to produce high performance. Lanier was highlighted for its service culture in the groundbreaking book *In Search of Excellence*: "Lanier and IBM typify the companies that go overboard on service among the high technology bunch."[10]

The popular book *Good to Great* missed the boat, however, in its analysis of the Harris Corporation (the company that eventually acquired Lanier in 1983). It missed both the long-term picture at Harris as well as the fact that Lanier, a large organization in its own right, was extremely profitable over a long period of time and was clearly a "good to great" story. How did *Good to Great* miss this success tale?

As the *Wall Street Journal* put it, "When Harris acquired Lanier Business Products, Inc. to create a word-processing business in 1983, it had all the makings of a disaster. . . . But this story took a different turn: The companies not only salvaged their union, they learned from it. Today, Lanier is Harris's most profitable unit. And Harris, drawing on its experience with Lanier, has grown into a diversified company with $3.4 billion in annual sales."[11]

The organizations that perform best and remain most profitable over time credit their success to a strong culture built on shared vision, mission, and values. During an in-depth study my firm made of what drove the public companies that were most profitable from 1972–2002, we discovered first that most of these organizations were not in *Good to Great*. These included top five, outstanding performers like Southwest Airlines (#1, and in a generally *terrible* industry), Wal-Mart (#2—how did *they* not get on a "good to great" list?), Intel (#4, up from essentially nothing in 1972), and Comcast (#5).[12] This omission resulted because *Good to Great* used an artificial definition of what constituted an organization that went from "good" to "great." In our consulting practice, we would much prefer that our clients look at the most profitable companies of the past thirty years—a long period of growth and performance—than at a company that had a relatively sudden spike in performance somewhere along the way. And a look at these great companies highlights the necessity of shared vision and values.

Cooperation and harmony are nearly impossible when there is no invisible glue of shared vision or values to hold a company together. We can try to substitute motivational speeches and tricks, but nothing superficial will do the job. If our teams truly share core values, however, we can focus on the major and not trip over the minor. Disagreement over direction or details doesn't feel like betrayal when we're of one heart and mind on the things that are most important.

The Japanese values of listening, study, continuous improvement, involvement, and collaboration produce excellent performance. But other values also sustain that culture: hard work, respect, and honesty.

One of the amazing things about the Japanese culture is the fact that hard work is such a distinct part of their culture. Whether a person is a truck driver, an engineer, or shoe-shiner, everything is done with genuine gusto.

There is one example I'll never forget. On one of my trips to Japan, I needed a shoeshine so I found a stand in the hotel. An elderly Japanese man was in charge of the stand. He was stooped, polite, and respectful, and he almost wore the shoes off my feet! I had never had such a vigorous shoeshine, and have never had one since. I believe his effort signaled something unique about Japanese culture.

Many executives have asked me if I would rather do business with a Japanese or an American company. The answer is easy. The Japanese are easier to do business with and they are honest. I can only remember one Japanese executive that I distrusted, and interestingly, he was demoted after a short period of time. It's telling that in Japan there are a lot of engineers and very few lawyers. The culture of hard work, respect, and trustworthiness makes lawyers less central to corporate life.

Obviously, non-Japanese companies should not try to become just like Japanese companies (a common fallacy that was pushed on leaders in the 1980s and early 1990s). It would be too difficult to implement many of Japan's approaches and processes without also having its ancient, homogeneous culture. And we don't want to lose the unique values of non-Japanese cultures—for example, the focus on innovation and raw creativity found in much of North America and Western Europe.

The point is this: Strong values make doing business relatively easy. People know where we stand. They don't have to spend time and resources protecting themselves and engaging in activities that don't add value. If people trust and respect one other and agree to work toward a common goal, they can devote 95 percent of their energy to creating value and only 5 percent to contractual and other potential problems.

Early in my career, I (Jim) was in a fairly responsible position in project management at Black & Veatch, a multibillion-dollar design/engineering firm in the power and industrial field. One day, I received an invitation to the office of N. T. Veatch, one of the founders, who was then in his eighties and essentially retired. He surprised me by asking what we sold. I started to talk about world-class engineering design and specifications. He listened patiently, and then said, "Wrong." Wrong? "We don't sell engineering services here," he said. "Our only product is trust. We want to do our work in such a way that no contract ever has to be pulled out of a drawer."

The principle of putting first things only—focusing on shared vision and values and bringing in people of character and competence—is essential to producing high-performance results. When we work toward a worthy vision, living our values and producing excellent results for everyone involved, we build the kind of trust that makes people want to do business with us. Those relationships sustain our success even when market realities start to batter our organizations.

> Many years later, apprehension and excitement gripped my heart as we flew at 35,000 feet above the Pacific Ocean. This was likely to be my last trip to Japan. The purpose was to close the deal with Ricoh, a huge organization, for the purchase of Lanier. After Lanier's spin-off from the Harris Corporation in 1998, it had become apparent to me that we could not make it on our own. The advent of digital products had greatly reduced our margins, and the spin-off arrangements had strapped us with hundreds of millions of dollars of debt and stripped us of cash.
>
> I wanted to sell to a manufacturer that could insulate us against margin erosion and that had plenty of room on its balance sheet for our debt. Ricoh was just the right answer to our dilemma.
>
> I already knew Sakarai *san*, the chairman of Ricoh, and we got along very well. As soon as I landed, we immediately

entered into hard negotiations regarding the price per share they would pay for Lanier. There were a few surprises, but I knew it was part of my final responsibility as chairman and CEO of Lanier to leave the company in good hands with a good chance of survival and prosperity. I knew from our previous experiences that our long-time Japanese partners would give Lanier that chance. After two days of negotiating, we finally reached a tentative agreement.

"First Things Only" Requires Transformational Change

There is much to be learned from the Japanese culture. They adopted many principles and grasped the significance of Total Quality Management long before we in the United States even thought it was a good idea. They capitalized on the work of Edward Deming and other quality experts.

The team-management process worked very well in Japan because they already had cultural humility. This *Kaizen* culture of making continuous improvements had become a normal state of affairs. Even though their products had once been considered cheap and of poor quality, with these principles in place, they began to excel. By the 1970s, their quality was world-class.

Edward Deming taught that 85 percent of organizational problems are systemic, rather than being caused by poor performers. Systems are often designed to get poor results—in many cases, perfectly designed. While U.S. and other companies were replacing people and looking for the next corporate miracle, the Japanese stopped making excuses and simply went to work putting first things only, completely redesigning and rebuilding processes. Upending an organization's culture and aligning it with powerful vision and values requires the humility to understand that change is vital.

My consulting firm has worked with Fortune 1000 companies,

large privately held organizations, and government and not-for-profit groups. Many tend to exhibit a common attribute. Unfortunately, it's not humility or passion or openness or competence or readiness to change.

It's arrogance.

Leaders who think they're the best have no reason to change—and *won't* change. They keep doing what they're already doing, which over time almost always means they're doing it poorly or wrong. They look down on the innovators, as U.S. auto and electronics companies did with the Japanese companies in the 1950s and 1960s—and amazingly, right into the 1970s and beyond, when the Japanese companies already had the upper hand in quality, process, and so many other bottom-line ways.

HPE leaders need enough confidence to know they can make a significant contribution, and enough humility to know that everyone can help them make it better. If our organizations could blend the confidence and exuberance of many Western organizations with the humility and steadiness of many Eastern organizations, we would have something very special indeed.

Summing It Up

HPE leaders start with the principle "first things *only*." They know that wrong priorities will never lead to greatness.

The organizational priority must be vision and mission first. We decide as a team why this organization exists and what it hopes to accomplish. Next, we agree on the activities that will most likely deliver on this big idea. Throughout this process, we keep in mind that results will suffer if the vision and mission are controlled by leaders to the exclusion of the people.

Right behind vision and mission is the priority of agreeing wholeheartedly with the organization's values, and then living them out with consistent behaviors. We define our values in a way that is coherent and practical, and then hold one another accountable to practice them without exception. Values with exceptions aren't values at all—they're merely good ideas worthy of a "nice try."

Once organizational priorities are in place, it is critical to bring people on board who demonstrate character and competence. If we find ourselves controlling and micromanaging people in order to obtain competent performance, we can assume at least one of two things: We have a bad ethic—or we have the wrong people.

HPE leaders design a culture and team that are able to achieve a clear, important vision and produce astonishing results. They know the central need is not for *organizational* design, but for *cultural* design.

It has been said that character is what you do in the dark. But it's more than that. Character is what you do *with* the dark. If we find that we are deficient in any area—vision, mission, values, behaviors, character, or competence—it's not too late to embark on a process of transformational change. This starts by carrying ourselves with what the Romans called *gravitas*, an unshakable seriousness about thoughts, words, and actions. What leaders prioritize becomes embedded in their organizations.

There's no excuse for putting off right things, and the best time to focus on them is *always* right now. "It's never too late to be what you might have been," observed novelist George Eliot.

Character is indeed destiny. If we get first things only—the *right* things only—we will be who we want to be, go where we want to go, and produce high-performance results in the process.

|||

DITCH THE DISTRACTIONS

You've got to keep your eye on the ball game,
not the score

TOO OFTEN, LEADERS focus on the objective rather than the mission, on performance measures rather than the critical success factors that create that performance, and on the score rather than the ball game. They concentrate on shareholder value, earnings per share, and profits rather than on the values, people, decisions, and actions that lead to those results.

When we focus on the benefits without understanding the costs of those benefits, we are on a perfect path to . . . nowhere. Greed (for money, power, fame, or anything else) inevitably produces poor judgment and dismal consequences. Either we don't get what we want, or we find that we really don't want what we get. Ultimately, there is no satisfaction in the distractions of greed.

In following the second principle of HPE, "ditch the distractions," we spend our energies building vision-aligned organizations that really serve stakeholders. We work thoughtfully and passionately to craft an organization that produces value for everyone—those who invest their lives (employees), their wealth (shareholders and investors), and their trust (customers, clients, and communities) in our adventure.

Instead of focusing on the results and forgetting to work on the process that produces those results, HPE leaders build a clear line of sight all the way from each individual's work to the ultimate achievement of the vision. These leaders act as conductors, coordinating each person's unique contribution into a harmonious whole.

This process starts with identifying factors critical to our success in fulfilling the vision and then creating a strategy to implement those critical success factors (CSFs). Next, we connect the work of individuals and teams to the organization's strategy and CSFs, and finally, we define and measure key performance indicators that will signify whether we are delivering on the vision.

Ditching the Distractions Starts with the Vision

The first HPE principle, first things only, lays the foundation for the second HPE principle. Before we can define CSFs for achieving the vision, we have to know what the vision is. Getting everyone focused on the vision sets the stage for defining our CSFs and the strategy that will implement them.

> Pebble Beach, near Carmel, California, is very beautiful in February—that is, if it isn't raining. My wife, Bernadine, and I had the pleasure of attending the Pebble Beach Golf Tournament on many occasions as the guests of 3M. The rugged beach, the beautiful trees bent into unusual shapes by the wind, and the beautiful homes all serve to give Monterey a spectacular vista. It was a place of dreams and a place where dreams came true, at least in 1986.
>
> That year, as Lanier's president, I had asked our friends at 3M to invite Dr. Joe Boyd, chairman of Harris Corporation (Lanier's parent company at that time), to attend with us. I hoped that by getting 3M's top management together with Dr. Boyd, we could talk about the future of our businesses together. I had learned that 3M was unhappy with the profits from their copier business, and especially with the lack of profits from their field operations.

Of course, field operations were all Lanier did at that time, and we were very good at it. In 1981, 3M had transferred all of its direct operations to us, except for major accounts. By 1986, I believed they were poised to sell us their copier business, and I was hoping that such discussions could begin while we were together in California.

On the night of the traditional tournament clambake, Phil Harris, a comedian who regularly appeared with Jack Benny on his radio show, sat at our table. He had been telling jokes and making off-the-cuff responses to whomever was onstage. We were all in a relaxed mood.

When I introduced Phil Harris to Dr. Boyd, I said, "This is Dr. Boyd, Chairman of Harris Corporation."

With a wry grin, Harris said, "Does this mean you're moving my --- out?" We all had a big laugh and enjoyed the rest of the evening, but I knew that serious discussions would be organized when each of us returned to work.

Those discussions began immediately, and soon negotiations for a 3M/Harris joint venture were in the works. However, as often happens during difficult transitions between major corporations, negotiations were tough. At one point, Jack Hartley, president and CEO of Harris, called me into his office to discuss the situation. Some of the Harris negotiators were discouraged, and Hartley seemed ready to throw in the towel on the whole idea.

"Press on," was my advice. "This is too valuable a deal to let go by us that easily."

We did press on, and for the first year, my boss Gene Milner served as the start-up CEO of the joint venture. I became CEO of Harris/3M in 1987. As we all began to work together, it became obvious that there were many problems. The company was divided, with employees remaining segregated along former organizational lines and lacking respect for one another. There were people who came from Lanier who thought their record in field operations gave them the right to be arrogant and throw their weight around. There were 350 people from 3M who were bright and capable, but they were used to a large corporate environment with many benefits and entitlements. And there were a handful of people who came from Harris and were accustomed to an academic/engineering culture.

Some of our top management people had developed the habit of putting down the 3M people at every opportunity. This caused us many problems, including a union organization attempt in our Chicago operation. I knew these problems and attitudes had to be addressed quickly if we were to succeed.

Unfortunately, there had been no vision process for the new entity. I now saw this omission as an opportunity to solve the intercompany rivalry and to install good principles at the same time. We organized an off-campus conference at Lake Lanier Islands so that we would be away from the day-to-day demands of the office. Inherent in this entire vision-building process was determining the purpose of our company. With the right purpose, it would be easier to get everyone in alignment and working in harmony. Everyone had to understand the purpose, and it needed to be the overriding factor in all decisions. It had to have universal appeal, and it could not be based on acquiring personal wealth.

For several years, I had dreamed of building the company on the basis of the "good name principle."[1] The vision of having a good name became a reality. We purposed to have a good name with customers, employees, and suppliers. We determined to have a good name with the spouses and children of our employees. We aimed to have a good reputation in the communities we served.

A good name, or any other worthy vision, is not achieved by simply being nice or not cheating. Vision is achieved by converting resources into greater value for people.

Ditching the Distractions Focuses Our Actions

In the process of aligning an organization, CSFs (mission) are the driving force behind achieving a vision. Strategy is the detailed but flexible actions that implement those CSFs, and we find that it's most effective to develop these sequentially (first vision, then mission, and finally strategy).

Developing strategies without a clear vision and mission, which is the practice at an incredible number of organizations, is a formula for suboptimal performance, strategic fuzziness, and eventual chaos. But by identifying the CSFs we will need to achieve our vision, we can put ourselves in a position to focus on our strategic options.

> At the new company's first strategic planning conference, we knew that the first and most important step we needed to take was to come to an agreement on one major issue: This company needed to capture all of the strengths and eliminate all of the weaknesses of each of the three companies.
>
> We knew this belief would offer value for everyone, regardless of his or her company of origin. At the start of the conference, we asked every participant to help us make a combined list of our strengths, an effort that invoked a good amount of spirited discussion.
>
> Then we developed another list, one of weaknesses, and talked about ways to eliminate each of them.
>
> As the facilitator, I led the group through an exercise to help us determine which strengths were important to the new venture and how we could best capitalize on them. The response to this exercise was quite enthusiastic; no one in the room could have imagined what a powerful organization we were bringing together.
>
> Next, we asked the group to come up with one thing about this new company that set us apart—a strength or characteristic that our competitors would have difficulty duplicating. We called this our "driving force." After much deliberation,

we determined that our driving force was our method of sale. We would focus on our unique strengths in bringing our product to the customer.

We knew that customer satisfaction was the most important critical success factor in fulfilling our vision of having a good name, but we wanted to move beyond simple satisfaction. We purposed that our new company would be the best in customer satisfaction compared to our peers.

I told the group about the time I had called on a customer in San Francisco and asked him what copier he thought was best. He told me that there were no good copiers; they were all bad in his opinion. "We just buy the one with the best service," he said.

I knew that most customers disliked the copier they currently owned, and the tendency to trade up for another brand was high. If we could keep our current customers satisfied and happy so they traded up for Lanier equipment, our growth rate would easily outdistance our peers.

Now we needed a strategy to implement our critical success factor of top-level customer satisfaction. Our advertising agency proposed a "far-out" idea: We would offer all purchasers a promise of satisfaction in writing, called the Lanier Performance Promise. We chose this idea as our strategy. Although this approach may be standard practice now, it was very radical at the time.

The guarantee would be substantial. We would offer to exchange at no charge any copier if the customer was unhappy. In addition, we would provide a rebate for any downtime exceeding 2 percent. We would offer to deliver a free loaner until we got the customer's copier back in order. And our customer hotline would be available seven days a week, twenty-four hours a day. Finally, we would guarantee the availability of parts, service, and supplies for a period of ten years.

I loved the idea because it gave customers real clout and assurance that their needs would be met, but I was concerned about the long-term cost. Such a promise would be a perfect reflection of our vision of having a good name. It would also support our mission of deep customer satisfaction. I was certainly willing to make a reasonable investment, but would our costs soar out of control?

One of our dealers, Rick Maxwell of Cincinnati, had long provided a similar guarantee for his customers, and he assured me that it worked without excessive cost and greatly enhanced sales. We also realized that we were already doing most of the things our Performance Promise would offer; we had simply never put it in writing or advertised it.

We agreed to give the Lanier Performance Promise a try.

When we decided to implement the Lanier Performance Promise, we simply intended to act on our mission of producing greater customer satisfaction. Little did we know that we would introduce an idea that would eventually become the industry standard.

To that point, the copier business had never enjoyed a good reputation in the market. All copiers were trouble-prone, and there was much deception in the industry. But now we were getting excellent equipment from our Japanese suppliers, and we felt that we needed to show our confidence in our products. This strategic guarantee supported the critical success factor of total customer satisfaction—and therefore fulfilled our vision of building a good name.

As a by-product, we also gained a good name with our shareholders because our growth and returns compared quite favorably to the best in our industry, even though profit was not the driving force of our business. We had seen the deceptive practices favored by the copier industry and we knew that commissioned sales representatives often moved outside the boundaries of ethical conduct in order to close sales. But with our emphasis on the Lanier Performance Promise and customer satisfaction, we also knew that these practices would not survive anywhere.

Lanier's leaders decided that the strategy of a no compromise performance guarantee would lead them directly to delivering on their mission of consistently excellent customer satisfaction. This then would lead them to the achievement of their vision of building a good name in an industry where a good name was hard to find.

Some critical success factors are common to all types of organizations. Lanier focused on one of the most common CSFs: a customer-centric approach that allows the customer to drive the process and have the clout. Other CSFs and the details of the strategy (in this case, the Lanier Performance Promise) will be very specific to the product. HPE leaders look for common and uncommon CSFs and act on all of them, because they know that carrying out a worthy vision depends without exception on this process.

The business of identifying and focusing efforts on CSFs might seem obvious when it is in print, but in reality, many organizations never take this step. Identifying CSFs and building a strategy to implement them must be done intentionally and thoughtfully.

Earlier in my career as a Lanier executive, I had discovered the importance of identifying specific critical success factors. One CSF for Lanier was helping our distributors recruit and train sales reps. Since sales reps were the major factor in our own growth, this made perfect sense. We conducted programs on recruiting and training new sales reps, and we offered training schools for their development.

We also helped our distributors identify their own critical success factors. We developed a template they could use to establish goals and detailed, step-by-step actions to hit those targets. We personally visited each dealership in order to help them build and implement a plan. We emphasized the relationship between a good plan and making quotas, and we offered incentive trips and lower prices on our products to dealers who met their quotas.

As a Harris/3M executive, I realized that other critical success factors were necessary if we hoped to fulfill our mission of total customer satisfaction. One CSF revealed by our customer surveys was short response time on service calls (the amount of time that elapsed from the time the customer called in until a service representative showed up to make the necessary repairs). We installed a central dispatch center so that we could measure turnaround time, and we required customer service representatives to call ahead to estimate their arrival time at the customer site. A related CSF was what we termed "first time final"—the representative had everything needed to complete the repair when he or she arrived at the customer site.

We also discovered that a CSF for customer satisfaction was guaranteeing the quality of copies produced. It was the nature of an analogue copier for the quality and contrast to slowly decline as the drum gradually wore down. Drums were expensive, so naturally there was some resistance to replacing them until absolutely necessary. Most of our customers had maintenance contracts that included the cost of replacing the drum, but our customer service representatives were on a bonus system based on profits. In this case, we realized that our existing incentive plan was counterproductive to producing customer satisfaction, so we eliminated the bonus plan and compensated our customer service representatives in other ways. Drums were replaced when they fell below specifications.

By the early nineties, we had made great improvement. Loyalty scores had risen above 80 percent, a huge improvement since our first measurement in 1988. We were moving toward our mission of being the best in customer satisfaction.

We started winning awards from our customers, which helped us earn the business of many new major accounts. In our quest to be the best, we eventually won the highest award in the copier industry—Buyers Laboratory's "Most Outstanding Copier Line"—in two consecutive years. This was truly remarkable since we were the first nonmanufacturer to win the award—we had assembled our line from several different manufacturers!

Identifying Critical Success Factors Requires Effort

HPE leaders spend the time and resources to define CSFs, and then focus relentlessly on making those things better. It is really easy to be lazy, to believe that a good product or service will sell itself, and that most people will magically work toward collective success. But there are few bigger illusions in business than the idea that "if you build it, they will come."

Without an intentional focus on doing right, organizations are ensuring that they will not do well in the long run. Wasting people and resources is both immoral and ineffective. But by doing right—taking the time to see what really adds value and ditching any distraction that destroys performance and squanders human lives—organizations have the potential to do very well. Studying our organizations with determination and humility and listening to those who have a stake in what we do gives us the chance to build high-performance organizations.

In the mid-nineties, one of our teams developed the idea of Customer Vision Week—one entire week devoted entirely to customer satisfaction issues and field trips for all home office executives to visit customers with sales and service representatives.

We put executives who normally didn't see a customer out into the field, where they talked one-on-one with customers and employees. The customers provided ideas regarding our products and service. During one Customer Vision Week, I called on a hospital in Corpus Christi, Texas. The administrator asked about our findings from our customer satisfaction studies, and I was able to tell him that Lanier ranked first, followed by Xerox and Canon. He smiled. He had all three brands in the hospital, and he told me he agreed with our findings. During our visits, we gave our customers awards, and they were surprised and delighted to receive recognition and gratitude from a supplier.

I loved getting out in the field. I enjoyed the people. As Yogi Berra said, "You can observe a lot by watching." By spending time with our people, I learned things that could have cost millions of dollars to discover. Each visit gave me insights and valuable information that I could use for promotions, policy changes, and company improvements.

I found that what mattered was not just the time I spent in the field, but what I did while I was there. I wanted to learn how the company did business and how it was perceived, why customers bought our product and how they used it. In order to gain this information, I needed to serve our employees while I was in the field, actually helping them with their work. I found that when I was transparent and open, they would open up and reveal the things I needed to know. By understanding the problems our representatives faced every day, I could build policies that supported the customers' and employees' needs.

We Have to Know Our Business to Build It

The essence of strategy is knowing how our business is working—and not working—at the point of contact with those who write us checks.

If we don't understand our critical success factors (CSFs)—what we need to do to achieve our vision and how our product or service can help our customers—we are destined for bleak results. To succeed, we need the self-discipline and passion to immerse ourselves in that practical information. If we aren't interested in doing that, it's time to find something else to do.

> Back in the mid-1970s, I spent a week with Lanier's Canadian distributor for dictation systems, conducting sales meetings, working in the field, and trying to unlock the reasons for their dismal performance. They were losing market share to Norelco, so I began asking the owner questions about prices, features, and how he planned to compete.
>
> The answers were surprising—although given his organization's performance, I suppose they shouldn't have been. He had limited competitive knowledge and no plan to improve the situation. He was spending no time in the field working with customers. As we say in the South, "That dog won't hunt!"
>
> On Thursday night, he invited me to dinner. Throughout the course of the evening, he displayed his vast knowledge of gourmet cooking, fine wine, and cigars. I suggested that he sell us his organization and go into the restaurant business.
>
> "Why would you say such a thing?" he asked, obviously surprised.
>
> "You know absolutely everything about food, wine, and cigars," I told him, "but you don't know anything about the dictating machine business." My response was calculated to shock him, to get him to pay attention to his business. I wish it had worked, but a few years later, we did buy that business.

Ditching Distractions Gives a Clear Line of Sight

Strategic implementation of an organization's CSFs requires a clear line of sight. Even with a clear vision, mission, and strategy, our people can become distracted by daily, relentless demands for non- and low-value activity. Our people need to ditch the distractions. They need a line of sight from where they sit, through all of the processes that surround them, to the strategy—and right on up to the mission and vision. If they can't connect what they do to what the organization does, the vision and mission and strategy will be nothing more than words on paper. If they don't know how the organization serves people or makes money, they can't help it do either.

When I ask people in my client organizations, "What are you doing that adds or creates value?" they frequently have no meaningful answer. Instead, they rattle off their roles and responsibilities. Roles and responsibilities often have little to do with an organization's vision, mission, and strategy. In fact, they may even be *opposed* to the vision.

A few months after our new Harris/3M mission and strategy were in place, Lance Herrin dropped by my office to discuss our national sales meeting that was coming up in a few weeks. Lance was general manager of our U.S. copier business, and he was quite enthusiastic about our new strategy.

He mentioned that the sales promotion company that was helping us with the meeting had a great idea for our customer satisfaction focus. "You're going to love it," he said. "You will probably want to use it for the entire company."

Then he showed me the preliminary artwork. The idea was to give this new focus a slogan and logo to drive the mission throughout the entire company. For me, it was love at first sight! The slogan was "Customer Vision" and it meant that we would see everything we did through the eyes of the customer and respond as a team to meet or exceed the customer's expectations. Like the Lanier Performance Promise, this slogan was a perfect reflection of our mission.

When we introduced it at the national sales meeting, I'm sure most of our people thought the slogan would be forgotten in a few months. That was not the case. We started to train our employees at every level within the company. In doing so, we all had to answer such questions as "Who is my customer?"

2: DITCH THE DISTRACTIONS

Some employees served internal customers, others served external customers, and still others served both. Our human resources department, for example, had every employee of the company as a customer. Accounting served both internal and external customers since accuracy of sales and production reports was important to our managers and accuracy of billing and invoices had a major bearing on customer satisfaction. Our service representatives and those who handled telephone requests served our external customers. By initiating major training programs and helping people in every department to serve their own customers well, we built clear connections between their everyday work and our organization-wide vision of earning a "good name."

The actual reality is dismal. In a recent survey, only five percent of organizations even tell their employees what their strategy is, much less involve them in strategy formation.[2] Excluding people from this central task scores low on both ethics (by devaluing people's "need to know" and ability to contribute intelligently) *and* performance (by allowing people to work on non- and low-value work because of management-induced ignorance). HPE leaders hate the dark and work hard to bring their people light.

We Need a Map with Mile Markers

We have to know where we are and whether we're going in the right direction. This process of ditching the distractions and focusing on what counts—so important in personal lives as well as organizations—must lead to results. HPE leaders need to know if they are actually implementing their CSFs and moving toward their vision.

We need to define and measure key performance indicators (KPIs) that will accurately tell us whether or not we are delivering on our vision, mission, and strategy. It's all well and good for leaders to say that they want a good name, and that they will gain it through exceptional customer service, but it's worse than useless if they have no idea whether or not they're actually accomplishing this.

Only the truth can set us free, but far too many organizations fear the truth, won't spend the energy to find it, and ignore it if it's unpleasant. They spend their time fixing blame rather than fixing problems.

The only way to know the truth is to ask hard questions—in surveys, interviews, focus groups, and other forums. These diagnostics provide the only way to know whether the mission and strategy are working to achieve the vision.

> In order to know where we stood, we had to institute valid measurement processes. In addition to key performance indicators like revenue and earnings growth, we needed measures of customer satisfaction. Most customer satisfaction surveys measure customers' perceptions of a company (the results of public relations efforts) rather than bottom-line questions like whether those customers will continue to buy the company's product. We decided that customer loyalty rates would be the key indicator of our performance in this area.
>
> To establish a point of departure, we conducted our first customer loyalty survey. We were shocked to discover that only 47 percent of our customers said they would buy from us again. We discovered that all of our competitors were in the same or worse position. It seemed that ours was an industry fraught with customer relations problems. Apparently, almost every organization hated its copier and was inclined to trade for another brand.
>
> This was a disaster, but it represented a major opportunity for us. We realized that this was our time to bring major change to the entire industry. The Lanier Performance Promise had been a good first step, but there was much more to be done. Through

company-sponsored training, our associates at all levels of the company learned better customer relations skills.

In addition to focusing on the satisfaction of our users, we knew we had to satisfy our internal customers—our employees. It's obvious that you can't be the best in customer satisfaction if your employees aren't satisfied. We needed to measure employee satisfaction just as we measured customer satisfaction. We were in for a rude awakening on that score as well. Our employees rated the company quite poorly, particularly in the area of communication. This score was difficult to improve, but we made progress. And we found that our employees felt very good about our customer satisfaction focus. Communicating that focus was one thing we had done well.

Through these efforts, we were able to improve our customer loyalty scores almost immediately.

In the early 1990s several independent customer satisfaction surveys were conducted in our industry. One of the most interesting was a Dataquest study that covered all major brands. At that time, Toshiba was our major supplier. The Toshiba brand was ranked eleventh while Lanier was ranked first—a very interesting result since the products were virtually identical. This proved to us that the quality of the product was only one part of the customer loyalty puzzle.

Faulty measurements enhance rather than annihilate illusions. Most employee satisfaction surveys, for instance, are so superficial, so removed from deep-rooted problems, so generic, and so unprovocative that they are useless in designing a powerful organization.[3] Senior leaders are made happy for a moment by the "positive" outcome—and then are left wondering why results are so meager if everyone is so happy. If we want to achieve a worthy vision, we have to think deeply and honestly. We need to identify truly important performance indicators and obtain thorough data to measure our progress.

Vision Alignment Produces High Performance

With a focus on the vital things, our organizations can reach the mountaintop of success, especially since most of our competitors won't be ditching the distractions.

> Back in 1974 and 1975, while the country was in a recession and our competitors were cutting their losses, Lanier had back-to-back record years with over 25 percent revenue growth in both years. This was so unusual that we received an award from *Sales and Marketing* magazine for our success in time of recession. The title of their article captured our unique achievement: It read, "A Funny Thing Happened on the Way to the Recession."
>
> The secret to our success was simple. We just kept doing what we knew how to do, in spite of rather dismal economic forecasts. We introduced new products, hired more sales reps, and launched new advertising campaigns. Since our competitors pulled back, we were able to make significant gains in market share.
>
> In 2002 and 2003, Lanier won the coveted J. D. Power Award for best customer satisfaction for black-and-white digital products. Even though I had just retired, this award meant a lot to me because it showed that we had achieved our purpose. Throughout this entire process, it became more and more obvious that there was a distinctive link between business ethics, customer vision, and bottom-line results. In every case, what we did was simply the right thing to do in accordance with our "good name" principle. And in the end, it paid great dividends.

Summing It Up

HPE leaders ditch the distractions. They keep their eyes on the ball game, not the score, knowing that if they focus on what counts, the score will take care of itself.

To achieve a vision (like earning a good name), everyone involved needs to help define that vision, invest in it, and aim toward it. In the Harris/3M joint venture, a focus on contributing strengths helped to undo in-house rivalries, which led to a shared vision. The best way to resolve internal warfare is not through conflict resolution, but by focusing on something positive about which everyone can be passionate.

With a shared vision, we can then define the mission—the critical success factors that will move us toward that vision. For Harris, 3M, and Lanier, one CSF was to create top-tier customer satisfaction. Getting out into the field and finding out what is really going on—and listening to those who are out there all the time—is the best way to identify critical success factors and know whether we're achieving them.

Once we know which critical success factors will lead us to our vision, we can create a strategy for making those CSFs a reality. The strategy (for example, centering the method of sale on the Lanier Performance Promise) is the plan for implementing the critical success factors (such as customer satisfaction) that lead to the vision (building a good name).

Once the organization is aligned—a strategy is in place to implement the CSFs that will lead to the vision—individuals and teams need to understand how to align their own work within the organization. They need a clear line of sight, which often begins with a question like "Who is my customer?" or "How can I best contribute?"

Surveys and measurements are vital to tracking our key performance indicators—and thus our vision. This means that our key performance indicators must be defined and refined in order to make any real difference to the organization's performance.

The result of eliminating the inconsequential in order to focus on the important is an ethical, high-performance organization, one focused on achieving a worthy vision and producing value for everyone involved.

ALIGN WITH REALITY

Never claim support for a bad cause

HPE LEADERS KNOW that aligning with reality is just as important in their organizational lives as in the rest of life.

In practice this means that there is an external reality that includes the core principles of human life. We can follow certain principles to produce positive results or ignore them to produce disaster—whether or not we believe the principles to be true (or even know what they are). Reality operates on the law that "we reap what we sow." Every decision or action produces certain actions and reactions; every change produces more change. Everything we do has consequences.

This external reality also includes the political and social environment, the economy, the market, our customers and non-customers, our employees and contractors, and our vendors and suppliers. These things simply are what they are, and guessing or wishing won't make them any different.

So this third principle, "align with reality," has two non-negotiable components:

» Aligning our personal character and the organization's culture with "big T" Truth—often called ethics or values

» Aligning with reality as a central component of HPE leadership (both a basic ethical principle and a key to high performance).

In the 1970s sitcom *The Bob Newhart Show*, Newhart played a psychologist who had a hard time controlling his group sessions. At one point, in the midst of chaos, he stood up on his chair and shouted, "I'd like to make a motion that we face reality."

HPE leaders second that motion, and then push for acceptance by acclamation.

Aligning with Truth Starts with an Ethical Example

The first component of aligning with reality is the process of weaving values deeply into the organization's culture. How do ethical values become integrated into the fabric of organizational life? How can we be sure that our people will "get it," and that they are aligning with enduring principles? The process begins when leaders set a principled personal example.

My relationship with Sartain Lanier began when I returned to Atlanta in 1966. I had been promoted to vice president and general manager of our dictating business, and our company was still a partnership owned by the Lanier brothers.

"Sot," as we all called him, was also chairman of Oxford Industries, a publicly traded company that manufactured private-label apparel. He had recently brought Carl Reith on board as president. When we merged the Lanier partnership into Oxford in 1969, Lanier operated as a wholly-owned subsidiary and we worked closely with Carl.

But it was Sot we worked with on acquisitions. In the early '70s we were on the acquisition trail and Sot's negotiating ability and knowledge of tax law was astounding. In one negotiation our adversary said to Sot, "You sound like a New York lawyer." Sot replied, "I take that as the highest form of compliment."

Sot's lifestyle was conservative and he didn't display his wealth at all. He drove conservative cars and lived in a nice home that was understated given his wealth. In his later years, I asked his wife how he spent his time. She said, "He counts his money." Then she looked me right in the eye and said emphatically, "Understand I said he counts his money—he doesn't spend his money—he only counts it!"

Sot hated unions and thought all taxes were excessive. At its peak, Oxford had over ten thousand manufacturing employees and never had a union, quite a record in the apparel industry.

Oxford was publicly traded and the accounting practices were conservative. Carl Reith preferred to use the term "realistic." There was no chance of overstating earnings or lack of total disclosure at Oxford because Carl and Sot set such high ethical standards.

I enjoyed a great relationship with Sot. In fact, on my thirty-fifth anniversary with Lanier (by that time, a subsidiary of the Harris Corporation), he participated in a video, a present for me, in which he said many highly complimentary things. What was the foundation of our relationship? Sot set a great example of high ethical standards, and that's where we found our common ground.

Rules Are Not Enough to Create Reality Alignment

In recent years, there has been a resurgence of belief in organizational ethics policies and codes of conduct. A quick look at a catalog of business ethics seminars reveals courses such as "Ethics and Compliance Program Management," with emphases such as "Risk Assessment," "Infrastructure," "Compliance Policies," and "Investigations." The catalog asserts, "The foundation of all ethics . . . is the company's code of conduct and compliance policies."[1]

Not likely.

The problem is that honor doesn't—and can't—grow out of a policy manual. It needs a deeper, more enduring source. In commenting on the Enron disaster, the *Wall Street Journal* noted, "Over the past three decades, the standard setters have moved away from establishing broad accounting principles aimed at ensuring that companies' financial statements are fairly presented. Instead, they've moved toward drafting voluminous rules that may shield auditors and companies from legal liability if technically followed in check-box fashion. But taken together, those rules can produce financial statements that present a distorted picture of economic reality."[2] This was written even before Sarbannes-Oxley legislation imposed additional rules.

HPE leaders base their internal covenants on something that has both lasting value *and* street value. They agree to an enduring set of values that guide their organizations and help them avoid ethical disaster while producing great results.

How do they know which values to use?

Ethics seemed to be the buzzword of the day during the 1980s and '90s, and I had read quite a bit on the subject. The question seemed to be how to decide on the source for the ethics of a company.

Business Week published a cover story entitled "Whose Ethics?" The questions were, who would decide what was ethical, and what was their authority for deciding? There seemed to be much confusion in the marketplace. Some companies surveyed employees to find out what they thought their company standards should be. Others used consulting firms to help establish codes of conduct.

Just ten years later, however, we saw that for many firms, ethics policies didn't make any difference. Every publicly traded company I am familiar with had some kind of code of ethics. But in the scandals that broke at the end of the 1990s, many good people lost their savings and their jobs as well. What had been the purpose of ethical standards in these companies? It seemed that most were nothing more than weak attempts to gain public support and admiration, and didn't reflect the deep convictions of the leaders at all.

What is to be the source and standard of business ethics? At Lanier we knew what the source of our business ethics had to be. A friend of mine, Col. Nimrod McNair, leads an organization called Executive Leadership Foundation, and he has helped many companies establish their ethical standards on the principles reflected in the Ten Commandments. In one of his meetings with executives from an extremely large company, he asked them if they could come up with a better source than these Ten. The management team was quite diverse, but they all agreed that the Ten Commandments were the best source of ethics and business principles.

At Lanier, we also agreed. We believed that realizing our vision of building a good name would require excellent performance, but it would also require excellent principles. So we built the Lanier Statement of Principles on the concepts we found in the Ten Commandments.

Sometimes minutely detailed codes of conduct can actually *eliminate* good decisions and behavior. When rules and regulations cover every potential action, trying something new or different—even if it could benefit customers or stakeholders greatly—simply becomes too costly. And yet, such rules lack any value when it comes to restraining selfish indulgence.[3]

HPE leaders focus on building deep commitment to enduring values. And they refuse to let people leave things undone that require a (perhaps painful) challenge to policies, procedures, rules, and regulations. HPE leaders know that it's just as easy to be unethical poor performers by leaving an important action undone as by taking wrong action.

Staying Aligned with Truth Requires Deliberate Action

All truly great companies embody the values that leaders live and breathe. But as time marches on, new leaders replace the old, or perhaps the company is bought out.

The leaders forget to teach the values, or they allow exceptions. They soften the language and expectations and they try to build a "bigger tent" so that more people will feel "comfortable." Sometimes they simply assume people will get the values by osmosis (a fatal illusion of great magnitude). Over time, values fade, drifting far from their original position of prominence within the company.

No one makes an announcement, "This value that we've lived for years is no longer applicable; we'll thank you not to follow it." But without constant vigilance, organizational entropy eventually decays once-ethical paragons of virtue, and values-drift turns well-run powerhouses into dark places.

Good ethics are so important that the principles must be intentionally taught, preserved, and passed down.

In the last few years of my career, I was greatly concerned that our company some day might forget our fundamental principles. We needed a way to communicate our beliefs and values to all employees. We needed these beliefs to be instilled at all levels in the company. We needed to make sure that all top managers embraced these principles and demonstrated them in their daily lives. I knew that we had to preserve the values for the future.

We began to create the Lanier Statement of Principles. We put together a team whose charter was to publish our business standards and create a plan for implementation. As the CEO, I sponsored the team and took an extremely active role in the process.

During the process of putting Lanier's Statement of Principles into writing, I interviewed Sot. It was amazing to hear him talk about the strong ethical standards he had in mind when Lanier was founded. I was pleased to know that these principles could be traced all the way back to the founders.

I asked Sot about the source of these principles. He looked very thoughtful and paused for a few moments before answering. Then he said, "I guess we got them from our parents." We taped his comments, which we then featured in our video used for training all employees on our Statement of Principles. Even though organizational success depends on constant change, we knew that beliefs and values had to be preserved and passed down or the company would eventually fail.

Stable and durable alignment must be staked on the only solid ground available—real values. Values that resonate in people's hearts and minds and make a difference in performance and prosperity. We need to build durable processes for passing those values to the organization's next generation. We need real, focused mentoring.[4]

It's simple: Values get passed down, consciously and conscientiously—or values die.

Aligning with Truth Takes Personal Courage

Preserving values over time often requires a little thing called courage. It would be nice if no one ever had to stand up for the truth, and everyone always did the right thing. That would be a great world.

But it is clearly *not* the world in which we are living.

We could say a lot about ethical courage, but here's the bottom line: It's less about being brave than it is about making an unshakable commitment to truth. HPE leaders are more afraid of *not* telling the truth than of telling it, of *not* standing up against a bad idea than of standing up against it. Fear can always invent a list of solid and practical reasons not to align with the truth.

But it's never the wrong time to do the right thing.

In a division of our parent company, an accounting procedure was used that bothered me. It was a complicated method for financing rental agreements. Even though it was legal, in my opinion it was misleading to the shareholders. Essentially, it was a tool that could be used for managing earnings. Rental agreements could be converted to sales on an as-needed basis.

It was an important enough issue that I decided I had to "put my neck in the noose," as I had on other occasions. Of course, I didn't recognize the politics of this situation, but I knew that top management had approved it. The division was small enough that its earnings were not material to the organization's earnings. But this accounting treatment allowed the division to be profitable on paper when in fact it was losing money. It gave a false impression to those who ran it, and delayed many decisions that would have otherwise been made. In reality, the division was a dying business that could only be harvested with a declining yield while a transition plan was implemented.

When I sat at the table with those who had made the decision to implement this policy, my neck was definitely in the noose. Luckily for me, a new CFO came on board, and he supported my opinion. God was definitely watching over me.

Taking a stand might be costly in the short term, but in the long run HPE leaders know that doing right—aligning with "Big T" Truth—is the key to achieving lasting success.

Aligning with Truth Leaves No Room for Untruth

The pressure to sell in a free market system can tempt even decent people to do indecent things. Outright lying—"Of course we always deliver on time" (when our on-time percentage is 75 percent)—is an obvious example. But "fudging" and rationalizing are more prevalent forms of deception, and they are perhaps more destructive because they are more difficult to see. I once worked with a sales manager who would ask, "Now, is this 'client truth' or 'true truth'?" He had a reality and an alternate reality, and sometimes got confused about which was which. We can get off the path of solid truth for so long that we no longer even know what it is ourselves.

Aligning with reality is more than not lying. It means telling the truth, the whole truth, and nothing but the truth. Within their organizations, HPE leaders maintain an unshakable expectation that everyone will tell the truth as a matter of practice. No one will make the truth into something less, either by leaving something out or by adding something in. "Say it straight or it comes out crooked," as the old proverb puts it. And as Abraham Lincoln observed, "No man has a good enough memory to be a successful liar."[5]

In 1988, shortly after we formed the new Harris/3M company, we identified a major obstacle in our quest to be the best in customer satisfaction and fully implement the good name principle: the issue of sales tactics.

The copying machine business was fraught with deceptive sales tactics. In many cases when we made new calls, the receptionist would ask the sales rep, "Are you a copying machine salesman?" The question was designed to get us out the door as soon as possible because customers remembered their previous bad experiences. This reputation was in direct conflict with our purpose of acting on the good name principle.

One common practice was to bill customers before delivery of the product. In some cases, the customer had not yet decided to buy the equipment! Frequently, sales reps would quote the customer payment terms that were far too generous and outside of policy. There were even cases of outright misrepresentation of product features and capabilities. Would we simply ignore these infractions because a sales rep "produced"?

We had to address this issue and correct it. First we dealt with our training for new sales reps. If we were to satisfy the customer ethically, we knew it had to start with the relationship between customer and sales rep.

We had to retrain our current sales reps as well. They had to understand deceptive behavior would not be tolerated. Unfortunately, we even had to end the employment of some reps as a result of our ethical stance.

We wanted to be known as the company you could trust, and it started with the initial contact with a new customer. We made great progress in this area and our customers often said that they bought from us because they trusted our sales reps.

Aligning with truth requires that HPE leaders answer questions along the lines in which they were asked. For example, if a customer or client asks if we *can* do a particular thing, that is very different from asking if we *have* done it. U.S. President Theodore Roosevelt said that the right answer to the question, "Can you do this?" was (assuming we have the passion, talent, and experience to do it) a resounding "Yes!" But if someone asks whether we *have* done something we haven't, the ethical answer is somewhere between "No" and "Not exactly, but we have had experience with these X things that will allow us to pull it off."

Aligning with truth also means remembering the important difference between positioning and spinning. Positioning is *placing* the truth in a certain light. It's more effective to say, "We are going to build a powerful strategy out of our experience and intelligence, while fully addressing any limitations we might have," than to say, "We've got to get past all of our limitations so we can build a workable strategy that might take us somewhere." Both statements talk about building a new strategy, and both talk about being realistic about limitations, but the difference in impact on morale and results could be great.

Spinning, on the other hand, is *replacing* the truth with untruth. It is an attempt to change a reality into an alternate reality—one that exists only in the false words of the speaker, and not in the actual world in which we live.

Finally, aligning with truth means that we tell everyone the same truth (the only actual truth). Salespeople have a reputation for telling the customer one date and then telling their own operations people a different date. "I know we'll be late," they say, "so we need to fudge the date." Then the scheduling people tell the plant or service center an earlier "must-have" date, and the managers there give their line people an even earlier date. If there is any "float" in the schedule, it's stolen or misappropriated. And this scenario occurs *after* the customer has already gone through half a dozen restructurings of their own "must-have date." How much money and energy get wasted by people trying to make schedules that aren't even real?

HPE leaders know the importance of squeezing the unrealities, partial truths, and outright lies out of the system. Just as strong business leaders have learned that information is an effective and inexpensive substitute for inventory, they also need to learn that truth is an effective and essentially free replacement for valueless—but extremely costly—activity.

Aligning with Truth Requires Action, Not Just Talk

All great leaders know that achieving vision requires more than just *stating* good values; it requires *acting* on the values and building organizational incentives to reward those values.

> When we introduced the Lanier Statement of Principles to our employees, we explained that promotion would be based on an equal weighting of ethical conduct and performance. In other words, we would not promote those who had great sales records but ethical failures.
>
> Our international business managers complained that some of our principles could not be maintained in their countries because of cultural differences. We understood that it would be

difficult, but we insisted that there be one statement of principles enforced throughout the company. Over time, our dedication to this commitment paid off in a stronger management team.

I can see now just how important the Lanier Statement of Principles was to our company. A number of international dealers even told me they came to Lanier simply because of our adherence to these stated principles. We hired quality employees who also felt strongly about and could support our principles. And our sales reps used the principles to provide assurances for our new customers that they could trust us.

All too often, values are nothing more than high-sounding words on plaques and Web sites. The only way to make them stick is to build them into the way we evaluate and value our people. If evaluations for continued employment, raises, bonuses, or promotions are mainly based on performance with only a slight nod to values, we can be assured that those values will mean close to nothing in practice.

Great results and an improving bottom line come from employees who get and keep the organization's values.

Aligning with Reality Means Surrendering Illusions

Aligning with reality includes one last important facet: surrendering illusions. A high percentage of leaders and organizations are "reality impaired." They refuse to face, define, and align with actual reality—about the marketplace, customers, employees, products, services, and competition—that surrounds them. Their thoughts and actions are clouded by myths, false perceptions, and ultimately the illusions that can be the greatest barriers to organizational success.[6]

In my research and consulting, I have been struck by the incredibly durable resistance many leaders and organizations have to obvious reality. They don't really know, perhaps, why employees come and go, why morale and commitment are sagging, why customers buy or don't buy, and why they aren't getting the results they want. They *could* know, if they have the courage. It can be difficult to face and align with the truth, but it is a crucial part of HPE leadership. We've worked with many leaders who have done it.

Illusions can often be fatal. For example, one of the deadliest cases arises from erroneous beliefs about the insecticide known as DDT. Since the 1962 publication of *Silent Spring*, the flawed book that led to a ban of DDT in the 1970s, its use has been drastically cut worldwide. As a result, as many as two million people (mostly young children) die from largely preventable malaria each year, with tens of millions dead since 1962, and hundreds of millions crippled.

This is in spite of the fact that a doctor with the American Council on Science & Health says that there "has never been a documented case of human illness or death in the U.S. as a result of the standard and accepted use of pesticides." Four decades of research show no significant threat to health from DDT, according to the British medical journal *The Lancet*. Steve Forbes has argued that the experts advising us not to use it have produced "one of the most immoral moves of modern times."[7] Still the illusion lives on, and still it produces fatal results.

Resistance to reality is even built into our language. The word "disillusioned" is in the dictionary, but "illusioned" is not (at least not yet; I had to create the word). But how can we be disillusioned unless we are first illusioned? Maybe we're disillusioned because that longtime customer left us. In all likelihood, the signs were there for a long time, and we were just too illusioned to see them. The truth *will* make us free, but only if we acknowledge its potential, its support of those who embrace it, and its destruction of those who ignore it (willfully or not). It's very hard to get premier results when we're misaligned with reality.

The two components of aligning with reality—practicing enduring, value-based ethics and acting in accordance with facts—are closely connected. When people try long enough to deceive others (bad ethics), they usually end up fooling themselves, too (fatal illusions).[8]

Aligning with Reality Produces High Performance

An organization that insists on truth throughout its value chain has a significant advantage over its competitors.

> I was visiting a customer in New York when she asked me, "Would you like to know why you are getting all our business?" Obviously I said yes.
>
> "Because you have the only sales rep that has never lied to me," she said.
>
> We could clearly see that our principles and our commitment to total customer satisfaction went hand in hand. No doubt our vision of having a company that built a good name by practicing excellent principles was a major ingredient in Lanier winning the highest J. D. Power Award in 2002 and 2003.

The upshot of aligning with truth is that honest tactics in sales also lead to increased performance and the achievement of vision. The dishonest approach might win a sale, but it also loses potential customers in the short run (those who see through the deceit) and paying customers in the long run (those who experience the deceit firsthand).

Does dishonesty sometimes pay? Sometimes, at least in this life, the answer is yes, of course. But it also diminishes long-term growth and profits, great relationships, a clear conscience, and rewards. It has to. Bad inputs yield bad outputs.

Does honesty always pay? Sometimes, at least in this life, the answer is no. But if we have good values based on timeless principles, we'll reap the remarkable side benefit of better results—better people, better partners, better vendors, and better relationships with better customers. HPE leaders know that the rewards will come when they focus on principles.

Summing It Up

HPE leaders are decent enough and savvy enough to know that full-fledged success will only come if they align with reality and insist that their organizations do the same.

The first side of aligning with reality is aligning with the principles of Truth. HPE leaders seek the whole truth and nothing but the truth, because they know that truth is sufficient. They are determined never to claim support for a bad cause, and just as determined never to claim bad support for a good cause.

Truth does not mean making lists of rules. Rather than an obsessive desire to be painfully meticulous in every utterance, truth is a core decision to align with what is right—making decisions that advance the good, and choosing behavior that *is* good.

The second side of aligning with reality is aligning with the facts. HPE leaders understand and accept that there are actual facts and real reasons for the things that happen. They know that excuses and rationalizations might make them feel better, right up to the moment that unaddressed reality causes disaster.

HPE leaders use mechanisms, tools, and forums to ensure that they constantly align with a constantly changing reality. That alignment may never be perfect—after all, we are imperfect and there is still so much to know—but the quest to find and embrace reality, and to hold on to it as it changes, is essential in securing the viability and long-term success of our organizations.

When HPE leaders decide to align with reality, and to hold their organizations to reality's standard, they are living this principle of high-performance ethics deeply and thoroughly.

The benefits will be exceptional now, and even better in the long run.

‖‖

FIND SYMMETRY

Without whole-life symmetry,
your life is on a crash course

HERE'S A REALLY unintelligent idea: Work like crazy without a break for thirty to forty years so we can do . . . nothing for the next thirty to forty years.

A good time-management strategy depends on grouping similar activities together in one block of time—but this approach should be applied to days or weeks, not to a *forty-year span*. Grouping all of our work at one end of life, and all of our rest at the other end, misses the HPE principle of symmetry and diminishes both work *and* rest. We're designing our lives to feel overused in the work phase and useless in the second.

Instead, HPE leaders find symmetry in every dimension of life.

"Work-Life Balance" Is a Terrible Idea

Let's be clear up front: This chapter is not about "work-life balance."

First, balance isn't the primary issue. We can be balanced—spending equal amounts of time in each area of life—but still burn out if we've missed doing the right kinds of things at the right times.

We don't need balance; we need *symmetry*, "a correct proportion of the parts of a thing . . . harmony."[1] We need a symmetrical life, with no component larger or smaller than it should be, a life in which everything fits well with everything else. We need the different parts of our lives to sing in harmony—diverse voices, one sound.

Second, the term "work-life" is a deceptive juxtaposition, for the simple reason that work *is* life. The very expression highlights the problem, as we contrast work with life, leaving us little choice but to associate work with life's opposite, *death*. We don't need work-life; we need *whole*-life.

HPE leaders don't strive for work-life balance, but rather for *whole-life symmetry.*[2]

If we denigrate work as the enemy of life and see it as a necessary evil, burnout is inevitable. Work becomes nothing more than something to get through as we look forward to weekends, vacations, and retirement. This view of work diminishes what should be a joyous part of life and exaggerates the importance of everything that is "not work."

Finding Symmetry Starts with Our Spiritual Dimension

Whole-life symmetry starts with tapping into our spiritual dimension and engaging our spiritual selves in our work.

> When Lanier was acquired in 1983, I continued as Lanier's president and also became a senior vice president at the new parent company, Harris Corporation. At Harris, my workload was much heavier than the one I had carried before the acquisition. The responsibilities I had at Lanier didn't change with the merger, but now I was also making thirty trips to headquarters in Melbourne each year. I was quite sure that I spent more time reporting than I did in solving our major problems. I quickly became discouraged.
>
> I was very open with our consulting psychologist about the situation. He was often a coach for those of us who found his

advice helpful. Since he was not an employee, he was free to tell us what we needed to hear and give advice that other associates dared not address. One morning over breakfast I told him how I felt about the relationship with Harris. He listened attentively and then said something that was totally unexpected.

"Wes, you're not using your spiritual dimension," he said.

Down deep in my heart, I knew he was right. For a Christian, burnout is often the result of saying yes to opportunities—even good ones—when the Lord does not approve of your direction. In this case, I had failed to make a connection to my spiritual calling, and I felt trapped in something that was out of my control.

When we don't engage our spiritual selves, the thing that makes us "us," we set ourselves up for burnout. Burnout can indeed result when work gets out of proportion with the other areas of life. But burnout is usually not the result of having to work hard or long. It's more often the result of playing a role that robs us of our spiritual connection to work. We know we're headed for burnout if we experience one or more of the following:

» We feel no passion or interest in the work, or our passions are not welcome
» We have too little, or the wrong kind of, competence and experience for the task
» Our work doesn't fit into a larger vision for our lives and our purpose
» We can't see the connection between what we do and a greater organizational goal
» We aren't able to contribute the kind of value we're capable of giving, or the type that the organization expects
» We deal with a constant tension between work and values
» We feel used by the organization or others
» We feel abused by leaders or coworkers

In these situations, burnout is more than possible, it is downright likely. We're *asking* for it. If, for whatever reason—lethargy, convenience, low self-worth—we've chosen to accept such conditions, burnout will take it from there and turn our lives into ashes.

Finding Symmetry Means Keeping Good Proportions

There will always be demands and competing priorities that we have to manage wisely, both to do our jobs well and to ensure that the important nonwork dimensions of our lives do not fail.

For many people, work often swallows up time that might be spent on other things. We allow this for a number of reasons:

> » *Fear of failure.* For most people, work is their livelihood and they simply can't afford to fail. But if we aren't careful, this fact can produce a "whatever it takes" mind-set—one that is driven by fear and worry rather than reality.
> » *Need for praise.* It's normal to want to be highly esteemed or to please others, and this desire often drives us to do much more than is required, sometimes even more than is sane. Mix in a little bit of perfectionism, and life can become impossible.
> » *Constantly changing expectations.* The organization, the industry, and the market are constantly changing, and if we want to keep up, it feels as if we can never stop.
> » *Unambiguous results.* Work is generally more linear than other areas of life. We can set goals and achieve them, we can make plans and realize them, and we have authority that is delineated and generally respected. This isn't always the case when we work with children, relatives, or other volunteers in the community.
> » *Respect.* Work is often rewarded with clear recognition and praise. But the payoff isn't always as obvious in other areas of life. (When was the last time your child thanked you for your impressive parenting skills?)

» *Significance.* It's very easy, more so in some cultures than others, to feel that work defines us. One of the first questions we ask when we meet someone new is, "What do you do?"

HPE leaders don't allow work to become the main focus of life. They aren't maniacs; they are *poly*maniacs: crazy about everything in their lives that has value. HPE leaders won't let any one thing take center stage, and they won't let anything get neglected.

> In my rapidly expanding business life, there was always a battle for the best use of my time. I needed time for business travel, time for my wife and children, and of course, time for work at my church.
>
> My boss was very demanding. Sundays and holidays meant nothing to him if he needed my time. Nevertheless, I recognized that my relationships with my wife and children were vital responsibilities God had given me.
>
> After I became CEO of Lanier, I was often asked by the press to name my greatest success. I always answered the same way: "My family is my greatest success."
>
> In the biblical qualifications for the highest offices in the church, leaders are required to have a reputation for ruling their households well.[3] Anyone in business knows how difficult it is to raise a strong family. In fact, unless we find a way to manage our time commitments, it's impossible. But what profit is there in great financial success if you wreck your own family?

It's easy to fall into the belief that we need to plan, organize, direct, and control our work, but that family activities will "just happen"— forgetting that much of what "just happens" isn't good.

But as tough as it is to be successful at work, being successful in the other parts of life can be a lot more difficult. We can't demote or fire our kids. We can't trade them to another team (tempted?) or send

4: FIND SYMMETRY

them to a foreign office. We don't get paid to raise them, and we can't quit. Someone has said that parenting is a job, but if so, it's hard to imagine who would apply.

Being a good parent (or partner, volunteer, or church worker) simply takes time, energy, commitment, and persistence. If we do it badly, a day will come when all of the business success in the world won't make up for the failure. How great is an impressive title if your son hates you? How wonderful is a pile of money if your daughter's life is a disaster?

More than "everything in moderation," HPE leaders want everything in *proportion*.

Finding Symmetry Means Cutting Extraneous Stuff

The biblical book of Ecclesiastes reminds us that, "There is a time for everything, and a season for every activity under heaven."[4] This highlights two critical points:

> » Regardless of how often people say, "I don't have time," the fact is we do have time to do everything we're supposed to do. It's finding the "supposed to do" and eliminating the "not supposed to do" that gives us enough time to do it all. This does not simply mean eliminating "bad" things; it also means eliminating good things that are not on our life agenda. The number of good things that we're not supposed to do is incredibly large.
>
> » There is a season—a specific time—to take care of each of those "supposed-to-do" things. If we're not careful, we can find ourselves doing family things during a work season, personal things during a family season, and work things during a volunteer season. We might be doing the right things, but doing them at the wrong time. We can't make that important business call if we're volunteering at school, and we can't help the kids with their homework if we're at the office.

Part of understanding HPE leadership comes from having the wisdom to step away from a good thing when its season has passed.

"Better one handful with tranquillity than two handfuls with toil and chasing after the wind,"[5] we're told.

Finding Symmetry Requires Asking Tough Questions

Finding symmetry begins by establishing some guidelines and asking ourselves several hard questions:

> » *Travel*—Will this trip add value equal to or greater than the energy and time I'll expend? Am I traveling for the right reasons or because I refuse to delegate, don't want to give up my visibility, or am trying to escape thinking or other responsibilities? Do I travel at times that match my "energy cycle" and allow me to be most effective? (I, for example, schedule trips in the middle of the day in order to accomplish things in the office before I leave and get to my destination before fighting rush hour, darkness, and exhaustion.)
>
> » *Meetings*—Do the meetings I attend (or allow) create value, or am I letting my time and other people's time be absorbed by largely useless conferences?
>
> » *Reports and reviews*—Do the reports I receive allow me to add or create value, or do they simply fill my mind with worthless data, give me information that really belongs to someone else, or satisfy my need to feel in the loop (or in control)?
>
> » *Mail, e-mails, and voice mail*—Do I treat these as tools (quickly eliminating the 95 percent of them that don't help and acting on the 5 percent of them that do), or am I a victim to a parade of correspondence that has nothing to do with high performance?
>
> » *Working on weekends and holidays*—Do I do this as an exception, when the current opportunity or challenge is so great that

I must put my all into it? Or do I do it because I have frittered away my time during the week, intruded on and micromanaged others, or tried to avoid an unpleasant situation elsewhere?

» *Vacation*—Do I view vacation as a mini-sabbatical that will allow me to recharge, reclaim, and reinvent? Or is it just one more thing to do, a time that's mostly occupied by worrying about work (or actually working)?

HPE leaders know that setting a good example in each of these areas will strengthen their own lives, and show others how to lead sound and satisfying lives that produce high performance.

Finding Symmetry Requires More than a Priority List

It's natural to seek a simple solution to the problem of an asymmetrical life, creating priority lists and pecking orders for our commitments. But this is not the answer to an asymmetrical life.

The key is to realize that if the things on our lists are the right things done for the right reason, they *all* comprise the good work we are here to accomplish.

> Until I received my first management promotion in 1962, my life had been divided into compartments. There was Wes Cantrell, the church worker. There was Wes Cantrell, the husband and father. And there was Wes Cantrell, the businessman. I didn't see much of a relationship between these three aspects of my life.
>
> After a year of total failure as a manager, I was humbled and more open to spiritual truth. When I first understood that God's Spirit was in me and that He had a purpose in every part of my life, it was a major breakthrough. I began to understand my calling.
>
> I realized that there was one driving force in my entire Christian life: God. The Lord was at the center of all activities,

and He had a purpose in each area that I was there to fulfill. Balance was no longer much of an issue when I began to see my life as a Christian as totally driven by His purpose.

I was a Christian who had been called to be a businessman. Just as my father had been called to preach and others I knew were called to be missionaries, I was called to the field of business. This understanding greatly changed how I lived my life, both at work and at home. I had a purpose in life: serving Him through business. This purpose was to drive every decision and be the basis of all my relationships with employees, customers, and suppliers.

Artificial priority lists are not useful for anything except producing guilt. A typical list might look something like this:

» God
» Family
» Work
» Church
» Community
» Self

But this type of list is phony and misleading. In the first place, spiritual realities should never be isolated at the top of a priority pyramid, but rather, intimately interwoven through all the areas of life.

Second, if we're going to be ethical, effective, and satisfied, we'll *have* to shift these priorities around, probably on a daily basis. Perhaps a particular event with one of the children is crucial to her development and our relationship; in this case, attending a church activity or staying late at work might be a low priority. But if the event isn't crucial, and there are important things to do at church or work, it might be out of symmetry to put children at the head of the list. It could even be unethical, for example to do poorly at work under

4: FIND SYMMETRY

the "family comes first" mantra. Sometimes, in fact, that decision is actually cowardly, if we're acting just to keep the children from being angry with us or other people from criticizing us as bad parents.

So today our priorities might be work-family-self-church-community, and tomorrow (or this afternoon) they might be self-church-work-community-family. The key question is not, "What should my priority list look like for the rest of my life?" but rather, "What should I be doing right now?" Life, people, and our own fragile personalities might lay guilt trips on us, but their priorities for us are irrelevant to what our priorities should be if we're living symmetrical lives.

As novelist James Michener writes: "The master in the art of living makes little distinction between his work and his play, his labor and his leisure, his mind and his body, his information and his recreation, his love and his religion. He hardly knows which is which. He simply pursues his vision of excellence at whatever he does, leaving others to decide whether he is working or playing. To him he is always doing both."[6]

Finding Symmetry Means Learning to Rest

Realizing that the results of our work really aren't in our own hands frees us to learn how to rest. Even type A leaders can learn to stop working, both in a spiritual sense—by setting aside the results of their well-done work—and in a literal sense—by doing something else.

The best lesson I've learned in this life was to rest.

In the late 1960s, my wife and I bought a house on a lake. Since I was so busy traveling and putting in sixty-hour workweeks, we knew that we needed a place to get away with the family on weekends. The lake house gave me uninterrupted time to be with the family. It was a wonderful retreat, providing us a place to play together, work together, simply enjoy being together. It was a place of rest.

In the Bible, the word *Sabbath* conveys rest. In the Creation, God rested on the seventh day—the creation Sabbath. In the

Law, the principle of the Sabbath was carried forward—the ceremonial Sabbath. I learned to rest in the power of the Holy Spirit—the Christian Sabbath.[7] We simply trust Him to do all the work and we rest in Him. When we enter into His rest, we cease our own striving and we depend on Him.

Authentic leadership places heavy demands on the whole life of the leader. But honoring the seasons and rhythms of life will extend rather than reduce that effectiveness—and can extend our lives as well.

Finding Symmetry Depends on Deliberate Stops

Whole-life symmetry is more than simply reordering our priorities at work. It means making good use of nonwork time. Harmony doesn't happen by accident, and the only way to maintain symmetry is focus on it.

HPE leaders designate part of every week as a pit stop—a time to ensure that the wheels won't come off the car when it's back on the track.

We loved our weekends at the lake. But we weren't sure what to do about Sundays. Should we stay at the lake and quietly worship God there, or should we make church attendance a priority?

With thought and prayer, our family decided we would return on Saturday nights so that we could attend church and participate in whatever ministries God had called us to do there.

Some of our friends thought we were a little strange for cutting short our weekends, but we were confident we made the right decision. Today, all four of our children are strong Christians and live lives of Christian service. And our twenty-two vgrandchildren are also following in those same footsteps. Looking back, I know that part of this can be credited to the high priority we placed on God's work.

There are some who honor a seventh-day Sabbath (Saturday), and many who honor a first-day Sabbath (Sunday). The important thing is not to argue about the details of the practice, but rather to *practice the practice*. Should we honor a seventh-day Sabbath or a first-day Sabbath? The answer may be yes.

HPE leaders know that we all need time for mental, emotional, and physical rest and for family. But we also need time for spiritual and social engagement, time for community and service. Using Saturday for one and Sunday for the other is one effective approach.

Maintaining whole-life symmetry arises out of regular pit stops.[8] How can we see whether the pieces are fitting together well unless we take time to look at them? We can only ensure that our lives are harmonious if we stop to listen to the music (or the noise).

Consider the following guidelines for effective weekly pit stops:

» *Leave work at work.* This ethical approach actually leads to higher performance. There is wisdom in knowing when to leave the field fallow so that it can produce at a higher overall level for a much longer period of time. The best creativity often comes when we're not in the middle of the insanity.

» *Remember that rest doesn't mean brain death.* If we think that resting means doing nothing, we're probably going to end up not rested (and perhaps even very tense) by the end of the day. Few people, and no type A leaders, profit from doing nothing.

» *Develop an array of refreshing activities.* This can certainly include golf or another sport we enjoy, but we'll need more than sports if we truly want to nourish our souls. We need activities—reading, music, events, hobbies—that relate to and expand upon who we are. And we need to develop a wide array of options so we'll always have something available to do.

» *Plan the time.* Most of us associate work with planning, and rest with spontaneity. But if you've ever watched a pit crew at work, you know that the time off the track is planned, organized, and effective—even though the car isn't running.

» *Know that giving can be refreshing.* Sometimes we think, "I've been working and working and working all week. I need a little time away so I can take a break from spending my energy." This line of thinking is understandable, but it doesn't relate to who we are as human beings. Refreshing others can be an amazing way to refresh ourselves.[9] Maybe a little time volunteering or encouraging a friend is just the ticket we need.

» *Realize that quality and quantity aren't opposites.* People talk about quality time as though it is unrelated to quantity time. The fact is, we might need to spend four hours doing something with a teenager in order to get the five minutes that change a life.

» *Allocate time for spiritual reflection and church.* Finding symmetry means allocating time to our spiritual commitments without either putting our spiritual dimension into a compartment or allowing those activities to replace (or take priority over) every other area of life.

Finding Symmetry Includes Redefining "Retirement"

HPE leaders know that it is crucial to mix regular rest with our work—and just as crucial to mix regular work with our rest.

Retirement, as it is generally understood, leads to wasted wisdom and experience, the trivial expenditure of valuable lives, and elderly people who feel useless in part because they haven't done anything useful in a very long time.

Peter Drucker, known to many as the "father of management," was professionally active throughout his retirement years and, at the time of his death at age ninety-five, was in the middle of writing a thoughtful series for the *Wall Street Journal.*

At his death in his nineties, the great Spanish cellist and composer Pablo Casals was preparing to conduct a symphony he had just finished writing.

Inspirational speaker Zig Ziglar has more passion and energy in his eighties than most teenagers on an adrenaline high.

We need to grow and change, not evaporate. The best life is one lived hard—worked hard, played hard, rested hard, and shared hard—from exciting start to fantastic finish.

> If it were up to me, I would rename "retirement." I prefer to call this exciting new phase "re-direction" or "re-invention."
>
> When preparing for retirement, most of us are well prepared financially. We solicit the help of experts, and we know how much money we'll need to save and invest in order to live comfortably. But we often neglect the one essential aspect of retirement: preparing for a complete change in our daily activities—and more specifically, our loss of identity. Business people often find their identity in their jobs. But when we withdraw from our occupations and conclude our professional careers, much confusion, depression, and even illness can be the result, unless true planning—re-invention—has taken place.
>
> Retirement can be an ego-depleting experience. As high-level executives, we were used to people agreeing with us, catering to us, laughing at our jokes, and meeting us at the airport. But suddenly, all of that is gone. After being spoiled with a private aircraft, now we're flying commercial. We look around and wonder, *What are all these people doing on my airplane?*
>
> Hoping to postpone the feeling of lost status, some executives linger after they retire, but I believe it is best to leave totally. Don't hang around or stay on the board—simply get out of Dodge! There is nothing worse than two CEOs battling over key decisions. This creates confusion for your associates and forces people to choose sides.
>
> So we need to leave, and that means we need to re-invent our lives when we retire. This is a time when we must come to grips with our purpose in life. Where do we find our identity? If

that key issue is confused, we could end up devoting the rest of our lives to golf or television or other leisure activities. Finding one's identity in a job or title creates nothing but trouble when you retire.

But if we recognize ourselves as Christ's disciples, here to fulfill His mission in life, then we are on our way to a happy and fulfilling retirement. If our identity is found in Christ, we never retire from that position—and no one can take that away.

As for me, I decided I wanted to "die with my boots on." I found that the only time the word *retire* is used in the Bible[10] is in reference to priests retiring from their regular duties in the Temple—the heavy lifting, if you will—and devoting themselves to other areas of service. They didn't stop working, they just did different things.

A Scripture I had chosen years ago to characterize my life was Matthew 6:33: "Seek first the kingdom of God and His righteousness and all these other things shall be yours as well." Since I've retired, the application of that verse continues to be my central purpose.

After the retirement decision was made, I puttered around for a month or so. But since that time, I've found so many great things in which to invest my time. There was no more work at Lanier, but there were many other opportunities that would have a lasting benefit to those served. I wanted to use the skills that I had learned as a professional manager and to do the service-oriented jobs that I hadn't had time to devote myself to in the past.

One of the first things I did was to prepare a fourteen-module course entitled "The Christian at Work." Whenever I teach the course, I am always amazed at the way young men and women soak up what I'm sharing. I've found that I enjoy telling stories about my experiences, and I especially like to help people understand that a Christian can be ethical and obey biblical principles while still being successful.

In addition, I now serve on several boards and am an occasional guest lecturer at Georgia State University, teaching MBA classes and mentoring some of the students. I've helped a group of Russian businessmen write a business plan for a start-up business based here in Atlanta. I was asked to head the development and building of a community playground at our church, and I've spent a lot of time with my grandchildren. Finally, I've really gotten to know my wife—and found that I love her more and more every day! A great advantage of being retired is finally having control of my time and calendar.

But just as it was when I was working, I know I have to use my time judiciously and keep everything off my calendar that doesn't aim toward my newly defined purpose in life. Thankfully, this is not difficult because I understand my calling as a Christian. Recently, my wife and I were driving together on the interstate when we passed the exit I used to take every day on my way to work at Lanier. My wife looked over at me and asked, "Do you miss working at Lanier? Do you ever think about it?"

I thought about it a minute before I answered. "No," I said. "I don't miss it at all." I love the people at Lanier, but I don't miss the work because my life today is so filled with fantastic projects that God has provided. I am grateful to Him. Retirement has been wonderful, and I know the best is yet to come.

Finding Symmetry Creates High Performance

HPE leaders find symmetry and realize world-class results in *all* of the dimensions of their lives. Whole-life success results from whole-life symmetry.

Every businessperson knows what it means to struggle with time management. But I learned that when you see your business as a calling from God, and when your family fully understands that calling, it is far easier to accomplish great things. Of course, any businessperson who uses this calling as an excuse to neglect his or her family or the church will pay a bitter price.

When we celebrated my sixtieth birthday, my son wrote me a letter of appreciation. In that letter, he said something about perspective that really struck me:

> *Dad, you were the consummate workaholic. But as strange as it might seem, for everything really important, you always showed up.*

HPE leaders know enough to observe days of electrifying rest. And whenever the important things are happening, they always show up.

Summing It Up

The fourth principle of high-performance ethics is about making sure that there is a rhythm to life. It warns us that without whole-life symmetry, our lives are on a crash course.

This principle begins with eliminating the popular but bogus idea of "work-life balance." Work isn't the opposite of life, and work isn't bad. It can become bad, but so can other areas of life like rest and recreation. If any single focus is made the main attraction, it will empty life of meaning and power. To have whole-life symmetry, HPE leaders do a number of things. They tap into their spiritual dimension. They keep their work in good proportion and don't allow it to be driven by false motives. HPE leaders cut out the extraneous stuff and ask themselves the tough questions about how they are spending their time. They understand that priorities are not a one-time list, but rather a fluid attention to all the important areas of life. HPE leaders have learned to rest, and understand the amazing restorative power of pit stops. And HPE leaders redefine retirement to mean "whole-life symmetry with a lot more smarts."

Far from being a distraction to success, whole-life symmetry is, in fact, a linchpin for success for anyone wise enough—and counter-intuitive enough—to see it.

This principle is partly about perspective. It tells us that accumulation (of money, fame, or power) won't be enough—not now, not at the end, and not after the end. We have to build a lot more into our lives if we really want to have "enough." Having been a CEO, as great as that is, is only one course in the feast of life, and it won't differentiate a person from others in the end. As the old Italian proverb reminds us, "Once the game is over, the king and the pawn go back into the same box."

The goal of this principle of whole-life symmetry? "When God gives any man wealth and possessions, and enables him to enjoy them, to accept his lot and be happy in his work—this is a gift of God. He seldom reflects on the days of his life, because God keeps him occupied with gladness of heart."[11] HPE leaders don't just want high performance—although their principles produce it. They want to enjoy life to the full.

||||||||||||||||||||||||||||||||||||||||||||||||||||||||||||||||||||||||||||||||||||||||||||||||||||||||||||||||||||||||||||||||||||||||||||||||||||||||||||||||||

RESPECT THE WISE

If you can't honor the savvy,
you're in the wrong organization

ONE OLD SAYING defines maturity as following the advice of older or more experienced people—even when they're right!

By respecting the wise, HPE leaders access wisdom that they can't gain any other way, at least not for a very long time or at a very high cost (and all too often *after* it's really needed).

HPE leaders are often successful and respected mentors in part because they are also great followers. They learn from their mentors and follow the principle of respecting the wise. And so they're even more worthy to be followed.

Every Leader Is a Mentor by Default

This principle isn't about only respecting people who are all-wise. HPE leaders respect anyone in a position of influence in their lives, and they follow their lead *whenever it's the wise, right thing to do.* Jesus told His disciples to follow the formal religious leaders of the day—even though they were corrupt—whenever they sat "in Moses' seat," that is, whenever they spoke truth.

People who are in leadership positions are mentoring the people around them all the time—for better or worse, in word and deed, and through what's unsaid or undone. They can't help it. People naturally model themselves after (or develop themselves against) those who have authority, power, fame, money, or charisma. Mentoring is the default position.

This HPE principle encompasses the whole range of leaders, including those who mentor by choice and those who mentor by default. Even bad bosses can instill something of value if we learn to deal with them well.

Only a Few Are Wise Mentors by Choice

In addition to my wife, two others helped me during times of difficulty in my career. I met George DeBenedetto in 1956 when he joined the company. We worked together and became friends. When I became district manager in Baton Rouge, George was based in New Orleans and was a regional sales manager for dictation products. I felt I could talk to him about any problem without fear that he would use the information against me or share it with others. George was an excellent mentor with no vested interest; he was a good sounding board and gave wonderful advice and encouragement.

The other notable mentor in my life was Carl Reith, president of Oxford Industries when they became Lanier's parent company in 1969. We also became good friends, and I found that Carl was willing to provide high-quality advice with no strings attached. He was always interested in my success, even years after he retired.

Both of these men meant a lot to me, both professionally and personally. Through their influence, I realized the importance of good mentors.

A true mentor is an experienced and trusted adviser. There is a lot to unpack in this brief definition:

> » A mentor is an *adviser*. Good mentors don't tell people what to do; they make suggestions, helping others work out their

own idea of what they should do. Mentoring means using informal authority, influencing people through power that is willingly invited rather than structurally mandated. It is very difficult for someone in a position of formal authority to be an effective mentor. It can happen, but it is an exception to the rule, and it is exceptional when someone can pull it off.

» A mentor is *experienced*. Good mentors are not peers with the same level of knowledge and experience. They know more—about one particular thing, or about everything. They might have more education in the school of business, or more education in the school of hard knocks, but somehow they've picked up the knowledge or street-smarts that we need.

» A mentor is *trusted*. By strength of character or skill with relationships (or both), good mentors prove that they are trustworthy. They won't use their knowledge of our defects to destroy us. Even while pointing out problems and blind spots, they make those they mentor feel bigger rather than smaller. The very fact that they are willing to invest in us, with no obvious return to themselves, bolsters our sense that they are people worthy of our attention.

Good mentors are usually mentors by choice. They know the power they have to influence others and the legacy they want to leave by doing it. They won't leave the development of other human beings to random encounters. They know that a well-placed investment of their time and wisdom will still be creating value years into the future.

Most Leaders Are Not Wise Mentors (Most of the Time)

Most leaders—even older, experienced, or powerful leaders—don't usually act as wise mentors. In most organizations, leaders leave mentoring to happenstance, enjoying the power that comes with their formal authority and forgetting that their power can be a tool for cultivating the good of those around them. In fact, even very wise mentors are still flawed human beings.

When mentors don't set a top-notch example, or when formal leaders focus more on power than on mentoring, we can at least learn what *not* to do. We can offer due respect to their experience and authority without putting them on a pedestal. But respecting the wise does not mean kowtowing to every leader's every whim.

Of course, families often face the same dilemma. Respecting our parents can be complex in practice. Some parents are wise mentors, and honoring them includes building a life on their example and teaching. Other parents use their position of authority selfishly or foolishly, and honoring them includes learning what lessons we can (with or without their intentional cooperation) and following their advice as long as it aligns with ultimate principles. In reality, most parents combine elements of wise mentoring and selfish misuse of power. Honoring them requires a mixed approach.

Respecting the wise in organizational life involves a similarly complex relationship between leaders and those who have chosen to follow their leadership. In the best cases, this relationship reflects the principles of good mentoring, which we should receive with gratitude and strive to practice in regard to others.

However, in most cases, the relationship between formal leaders and their people usually involves a complex combination of power, authority, influence, legacy, and the potential for abuse. Our approach to these leaders requires a shrewd mix of respecting their role and the way their influence can shape us for good—while learning from their example what *not* to do.

> It was a typical weekend in the spring of 1955, and I was wait-
> ing at the Greyhound bus station to go home. I was graduating
> from Southern Tech in May and I was extremely excited about

starting a career. I already had a few job offers including one from IBM that would allow me to stay in Atlanta.

While I waited for the bus, I looked across the street at the headquarters of Lanier. Remembering that they had written a letter to our placement office regarding technical jobs, I decided to make a "cold call." Even though my clothing (blue jeans and sweatshirt) was not appropriate for an interview, I decided that I would use the time profitably and take a chance on selling myself.

In just a few minutes, I found myself standing in the Lanier reception area asking to see the man who had written the letter to the placement office at my university. After a brief wait, I was shaking hands with Gene Milner. First impressions are important and Gene made a strong one. He was six-foot, five inches tall, rugged, and rough-hewn.

It was not long into our conversation before Gene had sold me on Lanier and convinced me that someday, this would be a company to be reckoned with. He also spoke of big commission earnings and that impressed me. After a little bargaining, I left with a job offer for a starting position making $325 per month.

Gene Milner's friends and relatives all called him Jikker. His older brothers had given him the nickname as a child and it stuck. Even though he was informal in his style, we all referred to him as Gene or Mr. Milner within the company.

Not only was Gene a big man but also he was large-boned and exceptionally strong. As a youngster, he learned that he could lick almost anyone, and he loved to fight. This translated into a tough brand of courage that carried over into his sales and business career.

He was fearless even in the face of overwhelming odds. He loved to challenge everyone, and that challenging and competitive spirit was a hallmark of his leadership style. Age did not mellow that love of fighting. After open-heart surgery, he welcomed a fight over an auto incident. Gene, in his sixties with a zipper in his chest, fighting on the street in Buckhead!

He was tough as nails, an extremely difficult boss who on rare occasions managed to act as a mentor. In any case, he had a forceful impact on my business career.

A Wise Mentor Is More than a Coach

Mentoring is not merely coaching. A coach is an instructor, trainer, or tutor. While coaches can be valuable, theirs is a limited role.

> Gene Milner's leadership style was most like that of a coach. He definitely had an agenda and usually used fear combined with big incentives to motivate people. I once asked one of Bear Bryant's old players about the legendary college football coach's leadership style. He said it was based on pure fear coupled with the hope of being a winner.

A coach develops job skills or leadership skills, while a mentor develops *you*. Coaches make you a better performer, while mentors make you a better *person*.

A mentor sees your future success before you do and expects you to keep progressing even when the going gets tough. When we find this kind of inspiration, something special can occur.

> Early in my career it seemed that Gene decided that I would be successful. He had confidence in me—always challenging me and pushing me to perform above others. This created some problems for me. Being known as Gene's favorite didn't win me many friends, especially with those he pitted me against. It was obvious that Gene loved internal competition; it was his main leadership ploy. But he also used other notable techniques.

Gene would say to me from time to time, "Wes, I drove through Hiram the other day and on the water tank they have painted a sign that says 'Hiram, Georgia, Home of Wes Cantrell.'" I knew he was spinning a tale because Hiram was so small at that time it didn't even have a water tank. Nevertheless, I loved Gene's comment because I knew it was his unique way of visualizing success for me. Gene had a narrow perspective: Success was the only option.

Gene used every opportunity to sell our products or to show how they could be used more effectively. At parties or sales meetings given by our suppliers, Gene wanted to influence everyone there, and he wanted me to do the same.

"Someday they will be working for you," he told me, "so start building your relationships now." Gene clearly had a long-term vision for my career.

I was only twenty-seven when Gene first discussed my becoming district manager in Baton Rouge. I knew that the failure rate for sales reps who became managers was quite high, so I asked Gene what would happen if I didn't make it as a manager. Gene's answer reflected his sink-or-swim philosophy: "In this company, it's either up or out."

Mentors Open Their Strengths and Weaknesses to Us

Legitimate mentors allow others to witness their lives. This includes the whole picture: their successes and strengths as well as their failures and weaknesses—and how they deal with them. They show us what they learned (and what they *didn't* learn), why certain things went wrong, and even what they contributed to the failures.

Whether we're learning from wise mentors who choose to be open with us or learning by observing "less-than-mentor-quality" leaders, we should look closely at their strengths and weaknesses, as well as how effectively they translate these qualities into success.

Perhaps the single most outrageous story in Gene's history was the one concerning an infamous Mailgram. Early in my career, there was no e-mail. If you wanted to get a rush, high-priority bulletin out to the field, the best choice was to use Western Union's Mailgram. Western Union set up company addresses in its computer and through a satellite connection, any Mailgram could be sent overnight to locations across the United States.

Near the end of the 1962 fiscal year, we were running somewhat behind our sales plan and Gene wanted all the reps in the field to understand what they needed to do in the final month of the year. He dictated the following Mailgram that clearly spelled out the mission:

> *To all regional, division, and district managers,*
> *I am counting on your tails being out in the field selling for the rest of this month and all of May. I don't want to hear nothing [sic] but that you are producing. Don't hire --- don't do nothing else. Don't fiddle with papers.*
> *Don't talk on the phone to your grandmother. Get the --- busy selling for the rest of this fiscal year.*
> *Lanier Business Products, Inc.*
> *Gene W. Milner*
> *Chairman*

This message reached our managers, but by some strange electronic quirk, it also went to most of the Catholic schools across the country. Can you imagine the publicity this generated? In the beginning, to say the least, it was not good. One Catholic nun, the principal of a school in Texas, sent Gene the following note:

> *Dear Sir:*
> *I assume this letter was incorrectly addressed and not meant for me at all. Besides the incorrect sentence structure, the language*

> *is not inspiring nor uplifting. I certainly will never recommend any of our graduates to work for your firm.*

But in his inimitable fashion, Gene liked to turn lemons into lemonade. He issued a press release and the story captured the hearts of people across the country. Most people saw it as a homespun pep talk that accidentally got into the public domain and of course, that's what it was.

One Sister in New Orleans marked up the Mailgram with corrections and sent it back to Gene. He sent her a note of thanks, along with a gift of one hundred shares of Lanier stock. In her response, she was gracious and said, "If you ever move your tail to New Orleans, be sure to come by and see me!" Gene loved it and enjoyed telling this story on himself for years to come.

It is excruciatingly difficult to learn from those who make excuses or blame others for their flaws. Leaders like this do have something to teach, but it's usually about what *not* to do. People who are too arrogant and insecure to show their flaws are also too petty to teach us much—except to avoid becoming like them.

Mentors Challenge Us to Live Our Principles

Mentors start where all good things start: with values. They know that character is destiny, and they want us to know it too. A wise mentor—or even a formal leader with a sharp eye—can be a tremendous asset to someone who is ready to grow. Even leaders with different values and those who normally don't bother to practice mentoring can help us to identify our own values and challenge us to live up to them.

> Gene definitely knew himself. *Fortune* magazine had interviewed us, and we were waiting anxiously to read the story when it was published. We were in Hawaii at a dealer meeting

when the magazine hit the newsstands, and Gene's secretary sent us a copy by overnight air express.

I was waiting my turn to read the article and finally, Gene called and said to come by his room and pick it up. I knocked, and Gene was laughing as he opened the door. Gene's wife had read the article and she had said, "Why is it that in articles like this, you always sound like an --- and Wes comes out smelling like a rose?" Gene's reply: "Because I am an ---!"

But Gene also knew me. Once in casual conversation, I used some inappropriate language and Gene noticed it immediately. He said, "Wes, you shouldn't use those words. It doesn't become you."

A mentor must have the freedom to point out the blind spots in our value system. It is too easy to be illusioned and even self-delusional. We might assume that our interaction with others is just fine, when in fact it is disrespectful and detrimental, and perhaps even obnoxious and destructive. We might think we are being honest and firm in negotiation, when in reality we're leaving out critical data or taking unreasonable positions. This is when a mentor's insight is invaluable.

But a mentor's efforts to point out blind spots won't work if we aren't listening. When HPE leaders are called on an ethical weakness or unacceptable behavior, they are open to listen and don't react defensively.

Great Mentors Don't Take Control

Great mentors are distinguished by their comfortable relationship with power. They let people do things on their own. They don't take control, but rather help others learn to use their own authority and influence wisely.

When George Washington led a fledgling United States to victory over the greatest empire in the world of his time, many urged him to become king. The defeated king, George III, asked an American-born painter what Washington would do after the war. He would resign all power and go back to his farm, the painter told him. "If he does that," King George answered, "he will be the greatest person in the world." Washington did just that. He was, arguably, the greatest person in the world in his time. And he mentored an entire generation of outstanding leaders.

Mentors help people to learn and grow into competence and responsibility, free to make decisions independently. They want us to be greater than we are, perhaps even greater than they are.

> Even though it was not apparent to me or anyone else at the time, Gene gave me quite a bit of freedom to make decisions. Once, a business coach asked me to list the last ten major business decisions our company had made. Then he asked me how many of those I made without consulting Gene. I was surprised to find that I had made eight out of ten without his involvement. Gene's dominant personality covered the fact that he had actually granted me more responsibility than I had realized at the time.

Respecting the Wise Means Giving Them a Forum

HPE leaders recognize that mentoring is too easily lost in the push for performance and results, so they intentionally formalize the process, both for themselves and for others within their organizations. They create mechanisms to ensure the regular and effective practice of mentoring.

Respecting the wise includes connecting them with people they can mentor. In great organizations, this connection is not left to happenstance. Mentoring must be part of our leadership model and our organizational design. Good mentors can make a huge difference in what our teams are able to accomplish, both by passing along vital knowledge and skills and by providing support to those they mentor.[1]

To build mentoring into their organizations, HPE leaders could use this next checklist to evaluate a person's qualifications to mentor others. (Or they might ask those being mentored to complete it.)

MENTORING EVALUATION

Rate your mentor on a 1–10 scale (with 10 meaning excellent and 1 meaning very poor). A score of less than 80 says, "Not a mentor."

____This person listens well and spends much more time listening than talking.

____This person asks probing questions to promote discovery and learning, rather than making declarations.

____This person guides rather than instructs, and demonstrates the importance of processing information, making good decisions, and doing self-corrections.

____This person challenges me to think for myself rather than pre-scribing solutions.

____This person observes a situation for a long time before provid-ing succinct feedback on behavior.

____This person provides honest and useful information about his or her own past experiences.

____This person assesses progress and gives input in an organized, systematic, comprehensive, and well-conceived way, rather than making constant, random suggestions.

____This person provides encouragement and hope.

____This person role-plays and provides opportunities to simulate new ways of talking and acting.

____This person is content to work behind the scenes, but is ready as necessary to step out and speak up for those who don't know their way.

If mentoring isn't being done in your organization, it can begin with you. And as soon as you start, mentoring *is* being done in your organization.

Respecting the Wise Means Showing Gratitude for Their Influence

Once we've found truly wise people who choose to mentor us, we need to show them our gratitude—because it's morally right, of course, but also because it's smart. Gratitude is often the only way to pay a person back for being there, and for being willing to invest in us.

If we are serving as formal leaders, we'll need to remove from our organizations anyone who is unwilling or unable to respect the wise. Even if the reasons are understandable, they have to go. The cost in lost transfer of wisdom and increased arrogance is just too high.

There's a Form of Respect Even for Unwise Leaders

HPE leaders respect the position of authority even if they can't respect the personality. There are no perfect leaders, but if they're in charge they deserve to be honored in appropriate ways.

What are "appropriate ways"? We should give them full attention and listen respectfully. We should question and challenge them, asking them to elaborate so we can see the full range of their thinking (and occasionally even get them to see the error of their ways). We can support them fully when they're right, even if we would do things differently. And finally, we can salvage the core of what they want to do even if we must first modify it for HPE reasons.

> Gene Milner hated our major competitors, and Dictaphone became the object of his disdain due to their sales tactics. In fact, the rivalry with Dictaphone became a driving force within the company. One night we had dinner with our Pittsburgh dealer at a well-known restaurant near our headquarters. As we were finishing dinner, we noticed a number of Dictaphone employees seated nearby. Gene said, "What are all those Dictaphone bums doing in my restaurant? Let's go over and find

out." As we approached their table, we could see the surprise on their faces. It was obvious they couldn't believe what they were seeing. Soon the surprised expressions turned to smirks as they bragged about their new product, known as "the tank."

The subject turned to the recently retired chairman of Dictaphone. Gene made some derogatory remarks about him, not knowing that he had died just a few days earlier. One of the Dictaphone executives became so angry that he was literally trembling, and he expressed his disgust. You might say that he rose to defend his deceased chairman, and the executive was visibly shaken. Realizing his blunder, Gene leaned over the table, took his own necktie in his hand, and held it out toward the defender. With a smile he said, "If I felt that strongly about something someone said, I'd grab him by the tie" (he was trying to hand the guy his own tie), "drag him out in the parking lot, and whip his ---."

Some of our suppliers did not particularly like Gene, either, but they all worked with him because our results were consistently good. In fact, we were at the top of most all standings as reported by our suppliers.

Gene could be just as difficult as a boss. He dominated every meeting he attended, whether or not he was in charge. Intimidating folks was his method of getting his way and keeping others off balance. Gene was emphatic in his use of profanity and his right to use it. Once he had dictated an interoffice memo to our word-processing center and they "cleaned it up." After proofreading it, Gene was furious. In no uncertain terms, he told them that no one was ever to edit any of his dictation unless he ordered it.

Sometimes working for this extremely authoritarian boss was very difficult for me, but I had to learn how to respond to him. Fortunately Gene had a great sense of humor and I sometimes pushed it to the limit. Once we drew an organization chart for the company and it looked like a wheel with all two thousand employees reporting directly to Gene. He laughed at it and told me, "The only reason for an organization chart is so you'll know who to fire when something goes wrong!"

Rarely did anyone receive a compliment from Gene. If you received one of his compliments, you remembered. His style was a pat on the back, but it tended to be delivered lower on the anatomy. Quick to point out mistakes and shortcomings, he seldom gave any encouragement. He demanded absolute loyalty and gave rare snippets of praise.

In short, Gene was demanding, insulting, sarcastic, and demeaning. In appealing to Gene, if I wasn't extremely creative, I took the risk of being verbally abused. I had to do my homework because he would always challenge my position. I had to learn how to respond effectively to his management style.

Does principle require us to work for someone like Gene Milner? No, absolutely not. But if we choose to do so, we have to find a way to respect that person and add value to his or her efforts.

Respecting Unwise Leaders Has Costs and Benefits

Every person in authority—even a "stinker"—can build something useful into our lives. One of the most frequent reasons people give for leaving organizations is that they can't get along with their supervisors. Unfortunately, they may be leaving a supervisor who is just the right "iron" to sharpen their own professional "iron,"[2] a person who might move their success to the next level. HPE leaders know that there is always something to learn from a person in authority—even if it's a lesson about how *not* to do things.

Recognizing this fact can provide a breakthrough way of thinking about unpleasant leaders.

It took a spiritual breakthrough for me to learn how to deal with Gene Milner. I found that in the Bible, the apostle Peter writes, "Slaves, submit yourselves to your masters with all respect, not only to those who are good and considerate, but also to those who are harsh. . . . How is it to your credit if you receive a beating for doing wrong and endure it? But if you suffer for doing good and you endure it, this is commendable before God."[3]

In reading other translations of the Bible, I realized that *harsh* could also be rendered *angry, surly, overbearing*, or *cantankerous*. When I read this I thought, *Surely Peter knew Gene Milner!* Of course, I wasn't a slave. I was choosing to work for Lanier, and I had the freedom to leave at any time. I owed Gene respect and my best performance—but not the unquestioning obedience masters demand from slaves.

Still, I recognized a principle for dealing with leaders. When we have done something wrong, we should suffer for it. We should expect it and take it without complaint. When Gene berated me for doing something wrong, that was as it should be. But if Gene treated me harshly when I stood up for principle and had done the right thing, the Lord was still pleased. This understanding made it much easier for me to work with Gene.

There might be enough value in our relationships with difficult supervisors to justify the ongoing wear and tear. In any workplace, we're going to encounter obstacles, difficult relationships, and imperfect leaders. But we need to look at the whole picture and ask, "Is this relationship causing me to grow? Is it worth the cost?"

If the value exceeds the cost, we may still need to set up some boundaries (or even barriers). It's too easy for a soul subjected to constant beatings to change for the worse, becoming either cowardly and subservient on the one hand, or tough and cynical on the other. The worst outcome is to become just like the flawed leader, treating people as we are treated rather than as we want to be treated. Respecting the wise does not mean copying our leaders' bad points or mimicking their destructive behavior. If we're at all wise, we'll learn to pick and choose—to see the good and see the bad, to know the difference, and to select the good.

Often the value of working for a difficult boss does not exceed the cost. There is nothing that requires us to continue working for a scoundrel, no matter how much he or she knows or has accomplished. We won't get extra points for career inertia, for taking beatings we don't deserve, or for supporting an organization doomed to failure by its oppressive culture.

If we can't in good conscience follow those whom the organization has deemed leaders, it's time to admit that we're in the wrong organization. Staying will only limit us, limit our leaders, limit the organization, and limit results all around.

Dealing with Unwise Leaders Takes Empathy

If we discover that the value makes a difficult work relationship worth the cost, then understanding the pressures our leaders are under may help us to deal with their difficult qualities.

> When Gene married Joyce, the daughter of Hicks Lanier, he was introduced to the business. At that time, he was in the electrical wholesale business and Hicks, recognizing Gene's sales talent, recruited him for Lanier. His first challenge was to move his family to Kansas City and open a new office there.
>
> The Laniers positively would not keep people on the payroll unless they were worth their salt, regardless of the relationship. Gene had to prove himself, even to his father-in-law. Being the boss's son-in-law was difficult and Gene took much ribbing about it throughout his business career.
>
> In later years, I realized that the family had put tremendous pressure on Gene, and I could tell that some of his direction

came from that pressure. Gene made no secret of the fact that his wife had the money in the family. And of course, the Lanier brothers had originally owned equal parts of the business.

At a dealer meeting in Hawaii, Gene was carrying on in his usual fashion, relentlessly kidding Joyce and making all kinds of exaggerated threats about what he was going to do. She was quiet for a long time, but finally she had had enough. She turned to Gene and said in her syrupy Southern drawl, "Let me tell you one thing, bustah—if you do that, the only thing you'll have left is two bird dogs, a sleeping bag, and a shotgun."

Gene loved her response and burst into boisterous laughter. The tension was relieved, and we all laughed with him. Having a great sense of humor, Gene saw both the truth and the humor in her comment.

Dealing with Unwise Leaders Requires Moral Courage

If we're not careful, a strong personality can transmit everything to us—the good, the bad, and the very ugly. If a leader has values different from our own, the gap is going to present huge difficulties.

But it is possible to honor our own principles and commitments in ways that add value to the work of the person with whom we disagree. In the long run, sticking by good values benefits everyone.

Many people wondered how Gene and I got along and worked together so well for so many years since our management styles and personal values were so different. Gene's definition of success was mostly based on making a lot of money. If someone made a fortune but neglected his or her family in the pursuit, Gene still considered that person to be successful. On the other hand, I believed that success was measured primarily on the basis of one's character and successful family relationships.

There were some things at Lanier that I could not do because I wanted to honor my convictions and commitments.

Although alcohol was often present at company functions, I never imbibed. During dinner meetings, Gene often explained to those we were negotiating with that between the two of us we had an "average drinking habit." Because I didn't drink at all, he had to "make up the difference." Often he would ask me detailed questions the next morning regarding the agreements we had made. This provided a good reason for me to be there and not drink: My memory was always clear.

Perhaps Gene accepted my differences because his father had been a Christian. He deeply admired his father, who was a Bible teacher and a successful insurance executive. He realized that there were actually some advantages to my being a Christian. He had certainly learned that my word was good and that he could trust me. He knew that I would always tell him the truth even when he didn't like it. Once he even referred to me as "Mr. Dependable." In an interview in 1984, Gene was asked why I had been successful. He said, "Every job I gave Wes, he did uncommonly well. He just stood out no matter what the job was. I don't like the concept that I selected Wes. I didn't select him. He selected himself."

Dealing with Unwise Leaders Depends on Shared Vision

Here's a key: If we're going to work with people with whom our values don't align, we're going to have to find some place where we *do* align.

Shared vision and fundamental business standards can provide needed common ground with an authority figure who disagrees with our personal values or has a flawed leadership style.

My common ground with Gene was found in business principles—we agreed on many. Such things as honesty, customer satisfaction, hard work, cost control, making a profit, and firing incompetent employees were important to both of us. The art of salesmanship and the importance of viewing it as a profession were also core beliefs that we shared. In all the important areas of business relationships with customers, dealers, employees, and suppliers, we had broad and general agreement.

Gene was a legendary leader; I often thought of him as the John Wayne of the office products business. We worked side by side for thirty years and I learned many lessons—good and bad—from him, lessons that had a profound effect on my life. I have an enormous sense of gratitude to Gene for the opportunities he gave me and for his confidence in me.

HPE Leaders Mentor to Multiply High Performance

HPE leaders don't rely on their position or power, but rather on what they can accomplish with those tools. Not only do HPE leaders seek out strong mentors, they also intentionally mentor others, passing along what they have learned.

HPE leaders often have the following objectives as they mentor:

» To help people plan their near and long-term futures

» To help people develop a good definition of success with a clear picture of victory

» To bring out the best in people, helping them to find their areas of passion and performance

» To impart a sense of vision and values to people, so they will know why they are here and what they can contribute

» To provide positive framing about the organization, so people are able to approach problems with an attitude that will allow them to create solutions

» To remove fear and develop confidence, helping people to take advantage of every opportunity

» To help people assume responsibility, take risks, and accept accountability

» To help people assume authority and find motivational resources to pave their own road to success

» To facilitate relationships and enable people to make the valuable connections that can improve their lives and careers

» To serve as an advocate who protects, promotes, and sponsors people, helping them climb ethically as high as they can go

Summing It Up

The truth of this HPE principle reminds us that if we can't honor the savvy, we're in the wrong organization.

The wise can help us catch a big vision for our own lives, perhaps bigger than the one we started with. They challenge us to live up to our principles, but they avoid the trap of taking control or responsibility for our lives. Good mentors are so important that HPE leaders create forums for the wise to work their magic in many ways with many people.

Every leader is a mentor by default, and we can learn something from every one of them. Much of what I've learned about leadership, I've learned from observing leaders in my own corporate career and from spending several decades working with leaders in my consulting practice.

HPE leaders know that there is wisdom locked up even in "unwise" leaders. They understand that respecting unwise leaders can offer benefits in the long run—if the cost isn't too high. It will take real empathy, great moral courage, and substantial common ground to pull it off, but if the value outweighs the cost, following a difficult leader is worth the effort.

HPE leaders become great mentors by choice. They understand the value of mentoring, make time for it, and use it to deliver high performance and a legacy for themselves. They know that mentoring includes coaching, but is also much more than that. And they have enough humility to know that they aren't perfect and don't have all of the answers. They are willing to expose their problems and weaknesses to shorten others' learning curve and make them more effective right now.

Wise people want to pass their wisdom along. Mentoring is "passing the Olympic fire" of wisdom. Those who see a strong runner approaching gladly take the torch. They carry the fire to the next runner, who can bear the flame into a distant future.

PROTECT THE SOULS

You can't climb very high on the backs of others

THERE ARE MANY ways to "kill" people.

We can kill their minds, their passion for work and life, their ideas, their careers, or their sense of worth. All too often, this occurs as a result of a leader's scramble toward the top—trampling others in the dirt, cutting them down and treating them as mere "costs" when the organization has market or financial challenges.

The alternative is the sixth principle of high-performance ethics: protect the souls. HPE leaders refuse to kill others in order to get ahead. They don't move their organizations forward through "body-count" thinking—slashing headcount, underutilizing or misusing people's talents, and manipulating other people's lives.

HPE leaders value others, and they build this same "others-first" humility into their people and organizational cultures. They know that developing respect for others starts from the bottom up. And they remember that no one is ever very far from the bottom—and that the arrogant are especially close to it.

Time at "the Bottom" Reminds Us to Respect Others

Almost everyone, it seems, would rather start at the top these days. This wasn't so much the case prior to World War II, but for baby boomers and their successors, the desire to start high has come to full flower. Western civilization's high regard for the individual has created a number of expectations that are far removed from knowledge, experience, and reality.

A good idea—respect for the individual—has developed some excesses. By treating the individual as a god and catering to the "it's all about me" attitude, many cultures have created a sense of entitlement among their people. Such feelings breed a desire to gain at others' expense rather than to earn a way up through ethical behavior.

The basement level is a good antidote to this attitude. People need to know that if they can't handle working at the bottom, either in attitude or performance, they'll never be able to handle it at the top. Their leaders will have to help them out with "remote career planning." Younger people need to understand the old saying, "Your opportunities, promotions, and raises will become effective when *you* do!"

In 1934 the Lanier brothers of Nashville, Tennessee, founded the company that still bears their name. There were three brothers: Hicks, Tommy, and Sartain. With humble beginnings, they started Lanier with less than one thousand dollars, and for their first business venture, they were able to secure a dealership for Edison wax cylinder dictating machines.

The Laniers were known for making gutsy decisions. The decision to sell dictating machines was one of those because the product was so hard to sell and there was strong competition from Dictaphone. Shortly after World War II, Lanier made another gutsy decision. They resigned from Edison and made a deal to distribute Gray Audograph in several southeastern states. Then they moved their headquarters to Atlanta. It was said that those who started businesses in Atlanta after the war simply couldn't fail unless they were stupid or inept. The Lanier brothers were not guilty of either.

In the late 1940s, they also bought Oxford Industries, a clothing manufacturer. They decided that Hicks would run the dictating business, and Tommy and Sartain would run Oxford. That was how the company was operating when I came aboard in 1955.

You might say that between the three of them, the brothers had it all. Hicks was a great salesman, Tommy was a people person, and Sartain was a financial genius. They made a great team.

When I started with the company, Hicks was Lanier's president and in control of the whole operation. Hicks was really "a piece of work," as they say. He was demanding and had a commanding presence. In addition, he was a dapper dresser and drove a Buick convertible. I was awestruck!

My first experience with Hicks Lanier was shortly after I went to work for the company. I was in the warehouse that was actually the basement of the building. With another worker, Jim Hall, I was checking out Gray Audograph dictating machines for shipment to Savannah to fill a large order. Hicks came storming into the basement and in a loud, hoarse voice he demanded to know "just who is checking out the units?" Russ Daniels, the shipping manager, pointed to us and said, "Cantrell and Hall, sir."

Hicks was obviously disturbed. He did not approve of the fact that Gene Milner had hired us, and he made sure everyone knew it. Gene Milner was the regional manager, but he was also Hicks's son-in-law and Hicks made every attempt to keep him humble. "I can't have those --- babies checking out my machines!" Hicks shouted. I never forgot that first encounter with Hicks.

Hicks was a great one for coming up with catchy sayings that really made the point. We were instructed to save the cartons for all products. In order to manage inventory, we shipped our product from office to office frequently. "Think big—but save the carton!" Hicks always told us. That phrase captured one of the most important lessons about success I was to learn from Hicks.

When I first went to work in Atlanta, I was told to report to the basement, where I was instructed to clean Mr. Lanier's fishing tackle. Evidently his boat had sunk and his tackle box was a mess. My first thought was, *This is an insult! I am a college graduate. I graduated at the top of my class. I'm too smart to be doing this. After all, I wasn't hired to clean fishing tackle!*

After thoughtful consideration, however, I decided to clean the tackle and to do an excellent job. It seemed to be the right thing to do since he paid my salary. In looking back on this event, I realize now that humility is necessary for learning. I wasn't nearly as smart as I thought I was, and this event clearly established the fact that I must humble myself and become a lifelong learner if I ever hoped to be successful.

That's a principle that I took seriously for my entire career. I believe Hicks Lanier thoroughly understood this principle and how it worked because he himself had humble beginnings.

Of course, none of us really wants to start at the bottom if we have a choice. But we should. The bottom can *teach* us as much as the top can *offer* us. The bottom is a good place to rest our wearisome egos. Why is the bottom so good?

- » *The bottom offers a look at the inner workings of the organization,* giving new or inexperienced people the opportunity to learn every aspect of the work.
- » *The bottom provides a safe beginning.* Expectations at the bottom are reasonable and employees don't have to pretend to know more than they do. There is nearly no way to fall, and there's nowhere to go but up.

» *The bottom builds confidence.* By learning to handle small things well and gaining small victories, we gain the confidence we need to move on to bigger projects.

» *The bottom teaches self-discipline.* At the bottom we have no past accomplishments, big titles, or political relationships to help us along, so we're forced to work hard and rely solely on the work we actually do and value we add.

» *The bottom teaches respect.* Because we remember how difficult it was to start at the bottom, we respect others who also start at the bottom and don't have power or prestige.

The alternative to starting at the bottom is to start at a higher level than we deserve, one that's higher than we're equipped to handle and doesn't teach us the nuances of life and work. This often occurs with celebrities who receive power, money, and fame before they've received wisdom and maturity—movie and television stars, musicians, athletes, and many of the people who have been handed the reins of power in family-owned businesses. Few things sound as ridiculous as celebrities who carry on about topics they know nothing about.

Starting too high is a superb path to arrogance, stupid decisions, and lost knowledge and skills. When immature people are told they're terrific, they begin to believe that it's so. They believe they are smart enough to hire the right people, invest in the right ventures, and say yes to the right opportunities. They also believe that the people doing the grunt work lack value—and can never teach them anything.

Starting low reminds us that we have *been* the people doing the grunt work.

Humility Prepares Us to Protect the Souls

Arrogance is a typical condition of the young, and some never lose it. Arrogance is always founded on ignorance—only someone who is ignorant about the size of life can be arrogant enough to think he or she has it all figured out. Arrogance is unaware of how little it knows and how naked it is. And arrogance, however youthful and under-standable, begs for a comeuppance.

> Some time after I was transferred to Gulfport in late 1957, Bernadine and I bought our first house. The office was in the back bedroom and I used some of the boxes I was saving as a desk. Eventually I sent a request to the home office for a real desk.
>
> A few days later the memo was returned. Hicks had used a black grease pencil to write in huge letters across the bottom, "Cantrell, the only desk you need is one out in the field—with a prospect seated behind it!" Needless to say, this message took me aback, but the point was clear and I knew something more about Hicks's personality.
>
> A few months later, when I called home for messages, Bernadine told me that a trucking company was attempting to deliver a large carton. They told her that if I would be home that evening, they would deliver it. We made the arrangements and I hurried home, having no idea what the package con-tained. When they opened the door of the truck, I was truly amazed. It was a brand-new Shaw-Walker desk. There was no note or explanation; none was necessary. I had just completed my best month to date, selling fourteen units. This was Hicks's wonderful and imaginative way of showing me the connection between my sales performance and getting the things I wanted. Nothing could have excited me more.
>
> In those days in Gulfport, I had no office equipment other than my inventory of products for sale. In checking my orders and making my expense reports I had to add up long columns of numbers. Once again, I wrote to headquarters requesting an adding machine. Once again, the answer came in that now rec-

ognizable black grease pencil: "Cantrell, I can add up all you're selling in my head! Best Regards, Hicks."

Hicks had a unique way of making his point, and it definitely helped me to keep things in perspective. Today's new college graduate would likely have been insulted by such messages and resigned. But Mr. Lanier taught me the humility and the self-discipline I would need to succeed later.

Humility provides more than a realistic assessment of ourselves. It also helps to build the character, self-discipline, and "others" focus necessary for great future success.[1]

Protecting the Souls Takes Confidence and Humility

Ethical behavior that values and respects others comes from a healthy balance of confidence and humility.[2] HPE leaders have enough confidence to know that they can contribute something unique, and enough humility to know that their contributions aren't perfect.

There is a fine line between confidence and arrogance. Confidence is knowledgeable, tempered, reality-based, others-focused, and inspirational. Arrogance is ignorant, overweening, reality-impaired, narcissistic, and discouraging. Confidence invites support and creates followers, while arrogance invites hostility and creates competitors. From success, confidence learns to do better, and from failure, confidence gains a competitive edge. From success, arrogance learns further arrogance, and from failure, it learns to blame others. HPE leaders do well to grow in confidence while keeping their feet well on this side of arrogance.

There is also a fine line between humility and debasement. Humility is self-deprecating, focused on improvement, and positive, building self-worth. Debasement is self-abusing, focused on deficiencies, and negative, destroying self-worth. Humility creates support and invites encouragers (and teachers), while debasement creates disgust and invites abusers. From success, humility learns that others must be involved, and from failure, humility sees new opportunities for growth. From success, debasement learns nothing new, and from failure, debasement learns that life is ugly. Humility, not debasement, comes before honor.[3]

Confidence and humility seem to be opposites, but in reality they are very closely interrelated and mutually supportive. Humility prevents confidence from morphing into arrogance, and confidence prevents humility from morphing into debasement. HPE leaders need high levels of both confidence and humility.

The right mix of confidence and humility produces healthy, ethical ambition and competition. Good ambition involves getting ahead without killing others. While keeping a savvy eye out for rotten people, good ambition views others primarily as fellow creators of greater value rather than as rivals. It creates healthy competition that raises every player's game to new levels (think Michael Jordan), rather than dysfunctional competition that pits teammates against each other and destroys their ability to grow and prosper. Ethical ambition watches out for the interests of others, rather than just for its own interests.

Unethical ambition fails to support, teach, or mentor others, and uses dishonesty and selfishness to get its way. It crushes others to get ahead.

> During my ascent to the position of Chairman and CEO of Lanier, many others also wanted the job. Most of them did their best to earn it through outstanding performance and the necessary skills. But there were some whose ambition was out of control.
>
> Three individuals come to mind when I think of this ambition run amok. These three men were all good presenters—persuasive, well-dressed, charismatic, and masters of making a good impression. In addition, all three were intelligent and accomplished enough in their positions to vie for the Chairman/CEO position. They had performed well, winning incentive trips and promotions, receiving a great deal of recognition, and basking in the praise they had earned.

The only attribute each of these men lacked was integrity. And without integrity, it's impossible to generate trust or to lead effectively. When these three started to believe their own press clippings, they jettisoned loyalty and regard for those above them. They were willing to do anything to move up.

In their attempts to discredit me, they were smart and subtle. I started to notice that their support for my leadership was restrained. They frequently questioned and second-guessed things that I said. Behind my back, they cleverly slanted their questions to discourage others from following me. When influential people are working against you, strange and illogical things will begin to happen, and reactions to normal situations will be unusual. I began to see these signs.

One of these men had used every opportunity to persuade the chairman that I was wrong for the job and that he would be a much better president. He had been so duplicitous that almost everyone noticed. But others were afraid to speak up because he had told many of our people that the job was his. The fact that he might get the job prevented their coming forward with the information.

After I had become president, when their misplaced ambitions and treachery became evident, I confronted each man individually. All three made outward shows of correcting their behavior, but I knew there was no inward motivation. As is often the case, it was actually impossible for them to see themselves as they really were. People like this tend to think you are wrong in your assessment of them and make only a surface effort to change.

I made a concerted effort to help each one of these men. When one of our top district managers resigned, he told me how one of them had mistreated him. With his permission, I recorded the conversation. Then I met with the accused man and confronted him with this information. The evidence was irrefutable. He was visibly crushed by this disclosure and went home that night in a downcast mood. I thought we had finally gotten through to him.

The next morning, he was waiting at my office when I arrived at work. But when I invited him in, he immediately began to explain why every accusation in the recording was inaccurate. He explained away the entire incident. His response made it clear that there was no hope of correction.

Once the offending parties were terminated, production immediately went up and so did morale. I learned two vital lessons from these men. First, we cannot tolerate treachery and selfish ambition, regardless of the performance of the offending individual. Bad attitudes are contagious, dragging down the performance and morale of the people around them. Second, the best solution is to create an organization where this type of individual cannot thrive.

Ethical Ambition Focuses on Value Creation

Good ambition combines a desire to move up with a commitment to adding value for everyone involved. Good ambition is marked by self-discipline rather than others-domination.

It was a hot September day in 1962 and I was very uncomfortable. I was also very excited. I was on my way to Baton Rouge for my first real management assignment and I could hardly wait. In that heat and humidity, driving a car with no air conditioning added to the sense of urgency. As I drove through Alabama and Mississippi, I was dreaming of what was ahead with my return to my old sales territory as the newly appointed district manager.

A few weeks earlier, I had been summoned to Atlanta from Augusta where I was based at the time. While there, I was interviewed by a psychologist. Both Hicks and Gene leaned heavily on these interviews to confirm or deny what they thought about the potential of employees. Although I was uneasy, I actually enjoyed the interview and found it to be encouraging. Since I had such a limited background and no managerial experience, it was helpful to be assured that I could do the job.

Gene had not been extremely reassuring, but he offered me the job. That in itself was some evidence that he thought highly of me. He again reminded me that at Lanier, it was either up or out. I was moving into a high-risk assignment. It was succeed or else!

As I drove through the countryside, I hardly noticed the scenery. Instead, I thought of many good salesmen who had failed when they were promoted to management. It was obvious that management required a different set of skills. The fact that a person is a good salesman in no way guarantees that he or she will be a good manager. However at Lanier, no one was promoted without a good sales record. Based on my good record I was confident I was ready for this new challenge, although I still had a mild case of anxiety.

One of the reasons I had stayed with Lanier was opportunity. I had seen that Lanier was moving fast and I knew I would have an opportunity to move up quickly. That observation was now proving to be true. But coupled with the opportunity to succeed was the opportunity to fail. My ambition and confident spirit would not allow me to be complacent, so here I was, on my way to Baton Rouge.

Unethical Ambition Leaves Others to Fail

Many people have used the term "blind ambition." There is indeed a certain ethical blindness about bad ambition—a blindness to long-term effects, a blindness to feelings and relationships, and a blindness to the destruction of one's own soul.

But moral blindness isn't the only cause of bad ambition. The other cause is quite the opposite: seeing what it wants *too* clearly. Unethical ambition sees the end results—sales, revenues, growth, profits, fame, or power—and it sees them with laser-like focus, creating an unending craving.

Ambition sees the ends, and it also sees the means. It sees the good means—study, personal development, role modeling, hard work, intensity. But it also sees the bad means—lying, cheating, manipulating, bribing, conspiring, backstabbing, shortcutting. Unethical ambition can't tell the difference between the bad and the good means—or else it just doesn't care. Bad ambition isn't simply a matter of ignorance or education, it's also a matter of bad ethics—and ultimately, of ethics that will destroy our own performance.

> When I arrived in Baton Rouge, I met the guys in the office, including my old friend Joe Bergeron, arguably the best district administrator in the history of the free world. Another one of the guys was the top salesman in the whole company at the time. He was an attractive Cajun, rotund with a quick smile and a good sense of humor. Although he was friendly and outwardly supportive, I would learn later that this was a misleading facade.
>
> My new boss was also there to greet me. He would be primarily responsible for teaching me how to be a manager. My reporting to him was to be short term. If all went well, this would be for a period of eighteen months, after which I would be on my own. My boss had an excellent record in the company. Young and single, he was very aggressive and smart and had won every incentive trip for which he was eligible. On a recent incentive trip to Acapulco, I had met him and the top salesman in the company, so they were familiar faces in my new Baton Rouge location. At that point, I was ninth in the company sales competition. In addition to the challenge of a new job, I would have to lead the number-one salesman.
>
> At one point, I had an argument with the top salesman. He believed that you had to lie during a sales presentation in order to be successful. This idea was abhorrent to me and I told him

as much. Little did I know that this was a precursor of things to come: I would eventually be forced to fire him for his deceptive behavior and for undermining the mission of the company.

For the time, however, my new boss and I jumped right into a close working relationship. My eyes of understanding were opened immediately. His values were also very different from mine. Although he was very smart about how things should be done, his personal values were about as far from mine as the east is from the west. We worked well together on the surface, but underneath there was little harmony. I felt no freedom to confide in him or share my fears and concerns.

At the end of each day, I struggled with doubts that I could do the job, and my boss did very little to encourage me in the learning process. I learned a few good skills from him, but mostly I saw management practices that I would never emulate. During my training he gave me very little support, no encouragement, and nothing to increase my confidence.

Up to this point, I had only worked in one- or two-person offices, and I had had no opportunity to observe good management practices. In addition, I was young and looked even younger. I had never seen a profit-and-loss statement, yet that was the basis of my compensation plan. With all this and a boss who really didn't care whether or not I was successful, discouragement was my constant companion.

Within a few months, it was obvious that I was failing as a manager. We were also experiencing great difficulty in selling our home in Augusta, and this only added to the pressure. My wife remained very supportive, serving as my confidence builder and confidant. Even so, I had an ever-present feeling of stress and fear of failure, a deep sense of unrest in my gut.

But failure is an excellent platform for learning.

Up to this point, I had never included the Lord in my business life. My life was divided into compartments, and He was neatly boxed out of my business career and our family. This is not to say I didn't adhere to Christian principles in business. I was very careful about honesty and ethical behavior. But I never consulted the Lord about business decisions. I had never considered that He would offer me His wisdom in every part of my life.

A wise person can still learn, even in the failure generated by the selfish ambition of others. For the intelligent observer, such poor behavior provides a very profitable school. This kind of behavior—even if it produces failure—creates an opportunity for learning to lead well, a lesson that can eventually bring great success.

But HPE leaders do not let their own ambitions blind them to the needs and success of those around them.

Unethical Leadership Destroys Others to Get Its Way

Many leadership models are unethical at the core. If our approach to leadership involves getting people to produce or keeping people in line by controlling or demeaning behavior, our model is wrong—even if we also invest in our people and prohibit dishonesty.

It is particularly malignant and murderous leadership that acts as though people are designed to be ruled and belittled, oppressed and abused. Ultimately, getting our *own* way means nothing. What matters is getting the *right* way.

My boss in Baton Rouge was not the only one who had failed to give me a model of good leadership. Hicks Lanier himself had often resorted to controlling behavior in order to gain his objectives as a leader.

Once, while he was having dinner with our Cincinnati dealer, Hicks was going on and on and complaining about bad conditions in our business. The dealer said, "If it's so bad, why don't you sell the business?"

With his daughter Joyce and Gene sitting right there, Hicks

answered instantly, "I would, but Joyce wants Gene to have a job." Gene's sense of humor kicked in publicly, but I knew this type of comment from his father-in-law bothered him down deep. Somehow he just couldn't win the Laniers' approval. Even with our outstanding results, it seemed that Gene never won their total stamp of approval.

By 1966, Hicks was relatively inactive in the business. Gene Milner was running the show, but behind the scenes Hicks remained a powerful influence. His grandchildren had given him the nickname Nero in reference to his extremely dominant behavior.

Hicks's dependence on control showed up in other ways, too. In the early seventies, Hicks bought a new car that wouldn't start unless the seat belts were fastened. He was most unhappy with this arrangement. He had a technician remove both the seat belts and the starter interlock so that the car operated in the same way as previous models. His comment: "No --- car is going to tell me what to do!" The people who worked for him sometimes faced the same leadership approach.

One of my firm's clients—the only one we have ever had to "let go"—forced its managers into a regular series of terrifying meetings informally dubbed "Stump the Chump." When I asked the CEO what his biggest issue was, he said, "Winning the hearts and minds of our employees." The senior leaders did not choose to see the obvious disconnection between their priorities and their goal.

HPE leaders praise publicly and criticize privately. Many leaders—and many parents—do the opposite, and it is an ethical and performance failure. Just because someone has the power to take cheap shots doesn't mean that he or she should. Doing so is cowardly, rude, destructive, unproductive—and wrong.

Protecting the Souls Creates High Performance

Ethical ambition gets good people working together to achieve success and add value. This kind of cooperation leads to high performance and promotion even as it also leads to the high ground of human relationships.

HPE leaders stamp out the notion of a bell-curve distribution of ethics and performance. They know that everyone in their organization can operate at a high ethical level, and that every ordinary person can do extraordinary things. HPE leaders want winners and believers, and they don't consider anyone to be "marginal" in any position in any part of the organization.

An ethical leader "simultaneously believes in using power and is keenly aware that its use is corrupting."[4] Power and ambition are used ethically when they liberate rather than dominate people, when they are seen as tools rather than as the goal, and when they work to the advantage of all, not just self.[5]

> As we continued to work the district, hiring new sales reps and technicians, things were going much better. I had put an ad in the Lake Charles paper for a sales rep. Only one applicant called in response to the ad. But that was all that was needed—he was a godsend.
>
> Cecil Herline had a background in teaching, and he knew many people in the field of education. The timing was absolutely perfect—Congress had just passed the Elementary and Secondary Education Act, making billions of dollars available to our schools for the improvement of education. As a result of Cecil's know-how, we were positioned to sell hundreds of thousands of dollars' worth of overhead projectors, transparencies, and copiers to the schools in Louisiana.
>
> Our business started to accelerate. We sold a lot of everything, including the new, revolutionary dictation system called Nyematic and the new dual-spectrum dry photocopiers from

3M. The results were simply fabulous, and the district sales revenues grew from four hundred thousand dollars annually to more than $1.7 million.

These outstanding results were the stepping-stone to my next promotion, moving back to Atlanta to become general manager of the dictation business in 1966.

It is possible to do well by doing right. And it is the only viable option for a well-constructed life. This requires an expanded definition of "success." The cheap definition is "getting what you want, however you can get it," a twisted version of the so-called American dream. A more robust definition would be "getting outstanding results through passion, clear thinking, competence, hard work, and high-performance ethics."

When we find ourselves working with others who share this robust definition of success, great results can begin to pour in. And great results are the basis of advancement and prosperity. We don't need to use dishonesty, control, or other negative means of advancement to achieve great goals. And in the end, we'll be very glad that we didn't even try.

Summing It Up

It's natural to want to be better than we are, to have more impact than we are having, and to produce greater success than we are producing. Everyone wants to climb from a lower to a higher place.

Is ambition good or bad? Yes. Is it healthy or unhealthy? Of course. Ambition is good and healthy when it enhances people and performance, and when it elevates to great ends by using right means. Good ambition doesn't boost people by settling for poor performance, and it doesn't boost performance by abusing people.

Ambition is unethical and unhealthy when it degrades people or performance, when it moves toward great ends by using miserable means, and when it produces bad ends because the means are dysfunctional (like dog-eat-dog internal competition, often encouraged even while management touts "teamwork" and "team spirit").

HPE leaders remember that they can't climb very high on the backs of others. It might seem that some people have pulled it off, that they've used others as stepping-stones and gotten away with it, but appearances are deceiving. These people are standing in a very precarious place. When they stumble—and they eventually will—they will discover how thin their ranks of support really are. Others might shout, "Long live the king (or queen)," but when they sense weakness, they will move with lightning speed to storm the Bastille.

Eventually—sometimes sooner, sometimes later—organizational destroyers leave the legacy of Attila the Hun. Of him people said, "Nothing grows where he has been." How ethical can it be to demolish decent human beings? How can someone be a hero for annihilating twenty-five thousand jobs? These scorched-earth, take-no-prisoners, my-way-or-the-highway leaders will be found out and disgraced, here or hereafter, because murder in any form is unethical.

War can teach many things, but it provides a bad analogy for dealing with others in life and business. In our organizations, no one needs to be killed for someone else to win. Because sooner or later, all of the casualties will take a marked toll on organizational performance.

HPE leaders only say what is helpful for building others up,[6] not for tearing them down. They remember the rule: "Love your neighbor as yourself."[7] And they consider others better than themselves.[8] HPE leaders fight against natural human selfishness and make their way to something generous, openhanded, and others-centered. In short, they protect souls.

No one is authorized to use or abuse other people in order to get ahead. No one has the right to kill another soul. As HPE leaders, we have to understand that we are dealing with valuable souls, and that we will find the greatest success by raising people from their knees—and placing them on our shoulders.

COMMIT TO THE RELATIONSHIPS

Without your partners, big wins are a pipe dream

IN AN ORGANIZATIONAL setting, HPE leaders make strong, effective relationships a high priority. They know the truth of novelist E. M. Forster's famous epigram: "Only connect."[1]

Committed relationships lead to high performance because new ideas emerge wherever even two or three skilled, passionate people are working together. And committing to the relationships is ethical because commitment to benefit others—both those in the relationship and those the relationship serves—is the most durable legacy and the highest accomplishment of any leader or organization.

HPE leaders invest in building this kind of relationship, even in that most difficult of contexts: mergers and acquisitions (M&A). They commit to the relationships and expect high performance to follow. In most M&As today, the commitment is to a shared interest (often a short-term interest), even at the expense of thousands of relationships. Not so when HPE leaders are involved.

In this chapter, we'll use the challenge of mergers and acquisitions to illustrate the relationship principle, although leaders encounter similar struggles whenever they try to form any kind of professional relationship. The work of every organization relies heavily on relationship—relationship with other organizations (joint venture partners, manufacturers, distributors, vendors, and suppliers) or with others inside our organizations (project teams, problem-solving teams, creative teams, interdepartmental or inter-business-unit collaborations, and normal daily work-flow interactions).

M&A is one of the biggest sources of relationship problems in business, both in the relationships it creates and the relationships it destroys. As we consider what it means to "commit to the relationships," we'll dig into what makes these difficult situations work—or not.

HPE Leaders Center Relationships on Producing Value

Blending disparate organizations and people effectively is very hard to do, and few do it adequately (much less well). It's hard enough to get human beings to build decent relationships in personal life. But it is doubly hard within and between organizations, especially since those relationships are expected to produce value.

> I was in the airport in Richmond, Virginia, late one evening in the early seventies, about to return to Atlanta. We had been busily running around the country trying to get everything to work as we had planned with three acquisitions. It required organization, reorganization, and many adjustments. I was traveling almost full-time.
>
> My name was called over the airport public address system and I rushed to a phone, not knowing what to expect. It was Gene Milner, calling to tell me that McGraw Edison had announced that day the sale of its dictation business. Gene wanted to know what I thought about it.
>
> I was very familiar with Edison Voice Writer and had competed with Edison for years. If we could acquire Edison, our organization and coverage would be complete, and we would pick up some great people and distributors, while getting rid of a pesky competitor.

My answer to Gene was quick and sure: We should acquire Edison.

In the years preceding this, we had acquired Gray, Stenocord, and Nyematic. In response to these acquisitions, *Forbes* magazine had published an article entitled "Tail Wags Dog," highlighting how unusual it was at the time for a distributor to buy out its suppliers. And now we had a chance to acquire our original supplier.

If an M&A relationship isn't going to produce value, it isn't worth the enormous tumult and expenditure of resources it will require. Often leaders delude themselves into believing that a hopeless M&A (or a hopeless team, or a hopeless interpersonal relationship) is going to produce value. Consider some of these less-than-brilliant, but often-cited reasons for initiating M&A combinations:

» *"We're failing and they're failing; maybe together we can succeed."* Think airlines. Think retail. Minus one and minus one may indeed have some synergy—it might add up to minus three.
» *"We see potential cost savings by combining operations and shared services."* Cost savings is not a case for good business. More often, the savings can't be found or manufactured, and all of the saving effort produces other consequences and costs that cancel out any potential savings. Then there's the impact on innovation, growth, and profitability to consider. After that first big cut (usually involving the elimination of jobs), where are the savings? What happens after the two CEOs leave or retire?
» *"Our product lines (or services) fit like a hand in a glove."* Nothing fits together perfectly. All combinations are painful in some way or another. Fit is a good reason to think about joining, but perfect fit is an illusion.
» *"We'll have a combined market share of X percent."* We also might trigger a consolidation in the industry that drops the organization down the list or even makes it a target for competitors.

» *"We'll double our (talent pool, R&D budget, resources, etc.)."*
One problem with this line of thinking is that we will also
double the market's expectations. Another problem is that
more input doesn't necessarily mean more output. We may
also double (or triple) our problems.

HPE leaders partner with others when doing so creates an organization with maximum opportunity for producing outstanding results, an
organization that capitalizes on the strengths of each participant. HPE
leaders require a good reason—a compelling, profitable-all-around
reason—for rearranging communities, organizations, and lives.

Successful Relationships Need Double Compatibility

Like all professional relationships, M&As depend upon two very high-
level, make-it-or-break-it factors: the compatibility of the two sets of
expertise and assets, and the compatibility of cultures and people.[2]

In my consulting with teams and on M&As, I've observed that
leaders always seem to consider only the blending of complementary
skills, assets, talents, and competencies. Seldom would anyone say,
"I think we should join together because our culture and values are
so compatible—I sure hope the business side has some commonality."

All three of the companies we had previously acquired were
operating throughout the United States, and we had different
distributors for each company in some of the same cities. Major
reorganization was required to rationalize our distribution.
To heap the McGraw Edison acquisition on top of these first
three seemed a stretch, but it was too good to pass up. I was
extremely enthusiastic.

We had bought Nyematic in order to settle a lawsuit. Several years earlier, we had developed some products to complete
their product line and offered these products to them. Our
idea was that they could sell them on a nationwide basis, but,

encouraged by a few underhanded Lanier employees, Nyematic decided to cancel our distribution agreement. We prevailed easily in the suits against the disloyal employees, but in order to settle the legal issues with Nye Systems, the best solution was for us to buy them since a lawsuit would have been more costly than buying them. Buying Nyematic gave us total control and settled all future issues that might have resulted in more lawsuits. It also gave us time to devote to business instead of to the courtroom and lawyers.

Both the Stenocord and Gray acquisitions had been driven by their desire to sell since they were losing money. Stenocord was essentially obsolete, so we acquired their distributors and installed base at a good price. Gray's product line was also obsolete except for the Gray ETC, a desktop that was compatible with IBM, the market share leader at the time.

No doubt the most important aspect of the Gray acquisition was the fact that the ETC was manufactured in Japan. It was an excellent product and its landed cost was surprisingly low—the exchange rate for the yen was 360 to the dollar at that time. We mainly bought Gray because we wanted access to their installed base and to Japanese manufacturing. The Japanese connection turned out to be far more important for our future. This acquisition gave us our entrée into Japan, which turned out to be the future source for most of our products.

We believed we were in a very strong position, and Edison seemed to round out all the remaining issues. The Edison acquisition provided total coverage of the United States, some very good people, and strong distributors in major areas like Cleveland and Indianapolis. In a real sense, they were strong where we were weak, and that's why the fit was so good. Dictaphone hotly pursued Edison, but the folks at Edison liked us much better because we were honest and direct. We promised to take care of their customers and employees and offer them continuing opportunities.

They liked us and trusted us, and they just didn't like the folks from Dictaphone, so we were able to make the deal.

Since Edison had the largest installed base, we decided to name the new product the Edisette 1977. This pleased all the Edison people very much. Now we had a powerful organization, hungry for exciting new products, and the timing couldn't have been better.

HPE leaders focus on the right things: how this new relationship will benefit the customers and clients. All too often during a merger, leaders fail to manage and promote the interests of customers and other key stakeholders. It is too easy to focus on the internal loose ends, distractions, and disruptions that are typical during M&A.

The second key element of successful M&A activity is the blending of cultures and people. Often, leaders' lack of "due diligence" in regard to assets and competencies pales in comparison with their lack of consideration about culture and people. "Of course we'll all work together and get along," they say. "Why wouldn't we?" This is a *fatal illusion*.[3]

Triumphant M&A—or team building of any kind—requires the successful blending of people and cultures around something they can share—a vision, a mission, a large objective, a new idea—something of value. Great new relationships don't just maintain morale; they *enhance* morale through the process of being formed.

The new product used the standard cassette. This was a break from the previous philosophy of the dictation business, which had relied on selling a proprietary medium of recording so that your company automatically received all the extension business. Since the standard cassette was just that, it would open our installed base to anyone who decided to make a standard cassette unit. But it was a pivotal time in the industry, and we believed it was time for major change.

We called our first national sales meeting, with the theme "Partners in Progress." All our distributors and district managers attended. It was an interesting time because the room was filled with people who had competed on the streets just a few months before. There was lots of excitement about the direction we were going together, and Gene and I gave fiery talks. There was no doubt that our troops were fired up and "wearing the same uniform" when they left that meeting.

In our product plan, we had planned to sell twelve thousand Edisettes in our first year. The distributors ordered twelve thousand units at that meeting, even though they covered only 30 percent of the United States territory (the rest was covered by our direct offices). We knew we had a real winner on our hands. We sold over forty-nine thousand units that year. This product and the people who came together to sell it were an overwhelming success, changing the entire industry.

Acting as one by focusing on a shared objective is one of the most important keys to success in any combination of human beings or organizations. Organizations mired in unproductive activity, complaining, and turf battles strongly indicate an absence of powerful reasons to collaborate. Nature abhors a vacuum. If nothing valuable fills the "space" between us, nonsense will inevitably pour in.

Just as leaders can be distracted on the operation and technical side from serving the interests of their customers, they can also be distracted on the culture and people side. It's easy to become so focused on sorting out all of the cultural disconnections and challenges that the real goal is also lost: to maintain and enhance performance and productivity during the transition. HPE leaders know that there can be no breaks from excellence in serving the market. They don't fret about the culture and people in *lieu* of the results, or even *more than* the results. Rather, they see integrating the cultures as the best way to *get* the results.

Successful Relationships Start with Good Foundations

Joining with other organizations in any type of venture is a risk. Under certain conditions, the risk is too high:

» *We've assumed complementarity that doesn't exist.* When we handle M&A or form other relationships, it's easy to believe there are complementary assets, products, services, or competencies when there are not. When creating teams, merely putting a lot of smart people with varied backgrounds in the same room will not produce value if there is no mutuality in the mix.

» *One or both organizations are crippled at the top.* Solid ventures require strong, focused leadership already in place. Forming a venture without strong leadership (or with strong leadership that has been distracted or debilitated) is a recipe for disaster.

» *We enter without influence.* Establishing any relationship involves negotiation. A position of strength is best. Equality is okay. But it is not okay to enter from a position of weakness. You will be taken advantage of and your ideas and ambitions will be scuttled, even if they are the best available.

» *We don't understand the venture or project.* Be wary of committing to or investing in a project that has no chance of winning. On the other hand, never close the door on something that could be the future. The key is deep knowledge.

These foundational difficulties are commonplace when it comes to mergers and acquisitions or team building, even within major organizations.

> We continued to pursue the acquisition of 3M copy dealers, and we were constantly talking to 3M about our future. The copier business was a natural for us. Since we had access to

product from Japan, I had pushed hard to take copiers nation-wide, but Gene was not enthusiastic about challenging 3M on this issue, so we decided to go into the word-processing business in 1976. With the advent of the personal computer in the early eighties, however, the word-processing business declined at a rapid pace. This drove us to look for a partner, which turned out to be the Harris Corp.

Shortly after we sold Lanier to Harris, we were operating as a wholly owned subsidiary and we made our worst acquisition. The Exxon Office Products acquisition was bad any way you want to look at it. The idea of one declining business acquiring another is analogous to two sinking ships trying to rescue one another. However, we thought we would replace Exxon's installed base with Lanier products as we had in the dictation acquisitions.

This turned out to be a bad idea. Exxon had no product that we expected to continue to sell, and the installed base was being replaced by the new IBM PC. Worse yet, Exxon's sales force was mostly ex-IBM and Xerox, and had been accustomed to large salaries and low requirements for productivity. Most of them left within a few months.

To compound the problems, Sartain Lanier was no longer working with us since we were part of Harris. Gene was our lead negotiator, and he had just undergone open-heart surgery and was not at his best. We had some help from the Harris staff, but we were beat at every turn by the slick Exxon lawyers. For example, we did not get a guarantee that Exxon would continue its service contracts with us for a reasonable period of time. As soon as the acquisition was completed, Exxon began to cancel these contracts and the revenue they generated disappeared. Since they represented almost 30 percent of the installed base, this was a major blow.

Finally, Exxon was in the fax business, a business we did

not fully understand. We could see that the margins, commission structure, and business model that was in place at Exxon could never make any money, so we decided to exit the business. But standards were being adopted for the fax industry and the business was poised to take off. In the past, each fax unit had its own communications protocol and would only "talk" to another unit of the same brand. Now this had all changed with the newly adopted standards, opening up the market to everyone. Without really studying the market and creating a new business model, we made a decision based on Exxon's business model. It was a costly mistake. It was the one thing from this acquisition that would have paid off and we missed it. Unfortunately, it is not uncommon for acquisitions to fail, particularly in technology-based companies. I recall reading an article in the *Wall Street Journal* that estimated that 90 percent of all acquisitions fail to meet expectations.

For any venture to be successful, HPE leaders must do *real* "due diligence." They have to look at root causes and drivers, and they need to understand the reality. HPE leaders ask the tough questions: Is there anything here that is uniquely complementary? Anything that is based on mutually reinforcing core excellencies?[4] No matter how good the idea, is our leadership available and focused to pull it off? Do we have the positional or structural strength to have our best ideas included? Have we analyzed how we might be hurt by getting into unfamiliar turf? Have we analyzed how we might be hurt by *not* getting into unfamiliar turf?

Successful Relationships Depend on Shared Vision

Building a human venture that works well is a rare occurrence. HPE leaders think about building on intangible ground—shared vision, mission, values, strategies—rather than only thinking of the tangible elements they can see and understand. The physical merger may make sense, but only if there has already been integration on less visible but more substantial ground.

> In the mid-eighties we began serious talks with our friends at 3M regarding the copier business. Joe Boyd, chairman of Harris at the time, went with me to the Crosby Golf Tournament as a guest of 3M. While we were there, we met Al Huber, the 3M executive for the copier business. Talks started immediately regarding the possibility of our purchasing the business from 3M.
>
> Negotiations were long and difficult, and the deal was finally structured as a joint venture. Gene would start the new company as CEO and after a year or so, I would move over as CEO of the company that was to be called Harris/3M. I was very excited as this company, a combination of Lanier's copier business and 3M's worldwide copier and fax business, would have revenues of more than $700 million. This was our second chance to get into the rapidly growing fax business. The fact that it was an international business added challenge and excitement.
>
> The deal was completed, and I moved over from Lanier to Harris/3M in 1987 as CEO. This was the most fun I ever had as a businessman. I was able to shape the strategy and direction of an entire company for the first time.
>
> To me it seemed that the key was determining the purpose of our newly formed company, so this became the core of our new mission. With the right purpose, I knew it would be easy to get everyone in alignment and working in harmony. It was then that we chose the "good name" principle as our vision.
>
> We also had to differentiate between profits and purpose. This is confusing to most people because there is so much emphasis on profits. If a company isn't profitable, it will eventually disappear along with the jobs of all involved. That's why profits must be emphasized. But the purpose of a company

must be something other than profit. Otherwise the result will simply be greed.

Profits can be likened to breathing. Everyone has some purpose in life. It may not be abundantly clear to everyone, but you have a purpose and it is not breathing. However, if you suddenly were unable to breathe, breathing would rapidly become your number-one priority. Profits, like breathing, are necessary to sustain organizational life.

The joint venture was very successful and generated lots of cash. In the early nineties, Harris decided to buy out 3M's interest on an especially favorable basis as outlined in the joint venture agreement. Then we recombined all that had been Lanier into one company called Lanier Worldwide, Inc. With revenues of more than $1 billion, it was operated as a wholly owned subsidiary of Harris Corp. It was destined to become Harris's largest and most profitable sector.

Joining at the right level and in the appropriate way—given complementary strengths—can help to circumvent some of the problems of an ordinary merger and produce great success.

It's too easy to think that the only good integration is a full integration—"If we don't fully merge these two organizations (or business units or departments or functions or teams), we won't get full value out of them." This leads to "rationalizing" the business.

But rationalizing might be less than rational, or might even be irrational. It could be that adding a physical merger—structural, process, and location integration—to the overall merger will actually *lower* the value of the connection. We might gain the intangible advantages of the merger, but we'll also gain all of the disadvantages of the physical merger (incompatible cultures, discordant values, conflicting structures, irreconcilable processes, and mismatched leadership styles). Or worse, all of the advantages might be obliterated by the forced physical merger.

Whether it's an organization or a team, focusing on what makes a good "whole" and leaving out any integration that doesn't contribute value is the only way to maximize collective victory.

Successful Relationships Require an Integration Plan

HPE leaders who are serious about success protect the new relationship with a well-thought-out map. After developing many of these plans with our clients, my consulting firm has seen the success they create—and witnessed the devastation that strikes organizations when they forego this important planning step.

> The most important factor in any acquisition is the integration plan. Without effective integration, the buyer never receives the full value. In some cases it may be best not to integrate but to operate the acquired unit on a stand-alone basis. That's exactly what Harris decided to do with Lanier. There was no business unit in Harris with which Lanier blended. The Street didn't like the deal. They couldn't see how the combination made Harris a better company, and the stock price reflected that thinking. Those of us who had stock options had our dreams dashed on the rocks in short order.
>
> Since we now had two word processors, we had to select which one we would go forward with. Although the Harris system looked good on paper, much of it had never been completed. It would take a big investment to make it a product. Lanier had a word processor we had developed and manufactured at our plant in Thomaston, Georgia. It was called the EZ-1 and had been mildly successful in the marketplace, but it had many problems. It was often referred to as the "sleazy one" behind our backs.
>
> We decided to have a face-off between the two concepts to help us decide which to go forward with. To my great surprise, the EZ-1 won the contest. It seemed that although Harris had much technological knowledge and was a great contractor for

> developing high-tech military products, it wasn't very good at
> making a competitive commercial product. This was one area
> in which we really needed help, and we were discovering that
> Harris couldn't help us.

Without an integration plan, organizations hoping to integrate with
another struggling organization are doomed. Alignment of excellencies and competencies is crucial, but it is often very hard to come by.

My consulting firm was approached by a growing training company that wanted to convert some of our most cutting-edge material
into standard packaged courses. As a firm with a primary thrust in
high-performance consulting, we had not developed the infrastructure of a typical training company and were wrestling with how to get
our advanced educational and developmental principles and practices
into the market. The training company had a solid infrastructure but
lacked any unique intellectual property. It looked like a "fit."

However, their approach required the reduction of ideas to a
"Management 101" level, so their trainers could learn it easily and
deliver it consistently. We felt the power slipping from our principles
and the cachet from our brand. We needed infrastructure, but not
that kind. So we ran for the exits. We built a new kind of infrastructure to support and take advantage of our unique principles and practices including licensing. It was slower, but a whole lot more effective.

Successful Relationships Require Facing Differences

Even if the value is real, problems stemming from extensive cultural
differences are bound to exist between two companies or teams.
HPE leaders accept the inevitability of this and face these differences
squarely.

> It didn't take long for us to understand the vast difference
> between the Harris and Lanier cultures. Harris valued knowledge
> and education. Many of its people had PhD's, and some even

demanded that we address them as "doctor." In recruiting, they put maximum emphasis on GPA. At Lanier we valued past performance regardless of education, and we didn't require a college degree for many jobs, particularly sales jobs. Lanier talked mainly about a person's sales results last month, while Harris often discussed someone's GPA. It was clear that ours was primarily a sales culture and theirs was an academic, engineering culture.

Harris meetings were very stiff and formal, usually running right on time. Lanier meetings were loose and spontaneous, taking more or less time on subjects as needed. We told jokes and demonstrated our enthusiasm for a project, while Harris employees were somewhat reserved. Harris was not very motivational in its management style. At Lanier, we gave many inspirational talks designed to inspire our people and we used incentive pay widely. This was not the practice at Harris.

Harris had a backlog of orders to be built and shipped. This was a large part of their reporting. At Lanier, since we were not manufacturing most of our product, we shipped and billed everything possible in the month we received the order. In one meeting, Gene told the Harris people that we didn't have a backlog at Lanier. He went on to say that we had a "front log," Gene's term for the fact that some overly enthusiastic sales reps often tried to bill an order before it was shipped.

Harris gave me a 40 percent raise. I had never received any raise like that in my entire business career, even when I became president of Lanier. By competitive standards, we were underpaid at Lanier and Harris was simply giving me a "catch-up" raise to get me on the same standards as their own people and the competitive world. This was another practice that had not been followed at Lanier. The tendency was to underpay family members because they had generous dividend income, and since my boss was a family member, I couldn't be paid more than he was paid. Harris brought to Lanier a much more sophisticated concept of compensation based on competitive wage rates and performance. But our emphasis on incentive pay for almost everyone was an especially new concept for Harris.

There was also the frugal travel policy at Lanier. We shared rooms, always flew coach, and rarely rented cars. Harris people always roomed alone, rented cars as a standard policy, and often flew first-class.

Clearly, it was going to be very difficult to blend the cultures in any meaningful way.

Is it really possible for cultures to clash over *travel policy*? Absolutely. In fact, there is nothing so trivial that it can't cause friction. Sometimes if the connection is unexpected and possibly unwelcomed, everything the other group does can be irritating, worthy of ridicule and undercutting.

HPE leaders assume friction on all points and are pleasantly surprised when there isn't any. They take great care to "clear the decks" on every point because they recognize that time spent on the front end will be nothing compared to the energy required to resolve back-end conflict.

Bad Relationships Can Be Improved by Honesty

For communication to work within relationships it must be honest, open, lavish, enthusiastic, and seamless. Everyone must get the same message, even if the amount of detail revealed varies from person to person. If any of these five elements are missing, the relationship is in trouble. In too many organizations and teams, all five are missing and can't be put in without a difficult intervention. HPE leaders find the blend of inspiration and fact that maximizes both communication and performance. They work to master the great paradox of spreading optimism and spreading the ugly truth.[5]

But communication is not enough. All parties need to be prepared to learn from each other and hear each other, to let their irritating differences reveal complementary strengths. Even bad M&As and teams can be improved and add more value when those involved make an honest effort to learn from the problems.

> The experience with Harris was a great learning experience for all of us at Lanier. We were exceedingly different companies, but Harris had skills that we desperately needed although we didn't realize that at the beginning.
>
> We saw Harris as an arrogant company, and no doubt they saw us as equally arrogant. We believed we were the best sales organization in the world, and we wanted everyone to know. Harris had little respect for sales, often referring to a sales pitch as "hype." They didn't believe in showing emotion, which is a key element in selling.
>
> But Harris brought to us much sophistication in running a large business. They had an operating human-resources function, not just record keeping as we had at Lanier. They employed sophisticated financial planning and skilled, knowledgeable financial people in each business unit. Planning was a major process, and all plans were reviewed up to the board level. The company required annual as well as long-term planning, all the things Gene hated. Eventually, we began to do a much better job of planning because our managers at Harris took a big interest in it.
>
> Lanier had never put much emphasis on financial management, except in regard to profits. All incentive pay was based primarily on profits, and we did a pretty good job in this area. However, cash flow, balance-sheet management, inventory management, and return on capital were issues that only our CFO took very seriously. These issues were somewhat new to us. It's not that we didn't know about them; we had simply never studied them or ways to improve them.
>
> Jack Hartley at Harris once told us that we were using "just

in case" inventory management rather than "just in time." All salespeople wanted everything in stock so that when the sale was made, they could deliver and collect their commission. This seemed perfectly normal to us.

Combining two groups offers tremendous opportunities for learning and growth. Each group simply needs to be willing to make a strong, honest effort to learn rather than disparage the other.

Good Relationships Mix Integration and Independence

In the final analysis, the goal of any business relationship should be to create higher performance than either party can create alone. This goal should determine the structure of the relationship. "Real listening means I allow you to change me," notes actor Alan Alda in his recent autobiography *Never Have Your Dog Stuffed: And Other Things I've Learned.*

Once, in studying the health-care market, Harris hired a consulting firm, Yankekovich, to study Lanier's reputation and opportunity. When I went down to headquarters for the presentation, I was pleased to hear them verify all the things I had reported previously. The consulting firm said, "Lanier has a love affair going with these hospitals." I was delighted, of course, but then, I had already told Harris the same thing.

It was about this same time that Harris decided to hire a consulting firm to determine what best to do with us, this maverick organization they had acquired. The consultants attended our meetings, interviewed our people, and made many field trips. I instructed our people to be open and show or tell them anything they wanted to know. I believed the truth would always be to our mutual advantage.

Much good information was brought to light by these studies, and they were unbiased in their recommendation. They convinced Harris that we were a totally different type of organization than Harris and that any forced integration of our companies would end in disaster. They were exactly right because the cultures were so radically different.

Keeping two companies unmerged, even after an acquisition, sometimes makes more sense than forcing a fit between incompatible organizations. Keeping two teams distinct can be just as smart.

It's been said that you can't force love. Neither can you force collaboration, cooperation, and mutual respect. Everyone involved must see the potential in order for a merger to work. If it isn't there, there is no reason to acquire or form a team.

But that initial decision is only a piece of the puzzle, and often it's a small piece. Leaders must be able to see how that potential can be tapped, and how best to do it with the people who are currently in the organization.

Often, HPE leaders protect the relationship by valuing distance as much as they value connection.

Committing to Relationships Applies to Internal Teams

In this chapter, we've focused on building partnerships within relationships, using the merger of organizations as a reference point. We can also apply this important HPE principle to internal teamwork and teams.

Although teamwork is an effective way to build a successful organization, management expert Peter Drucker long argued that almost all teams fail at some level. The basic problem is that most teams are built on the wrong principles. Team leaders (or those assigning people to teams) at best look for people who bring the right "skill sets" to the team, and at worst look for people who will do what they're told, are easy to get along with, and have the right connections. It is possible to build a successful team that creates enduring results. But doing so depends on several essential qualities:

7: COMMIT TO THE RELATIONSHIPS

» *Overtly conflicting competencies.* HPE leaders put people together who have different experiences, knowledge, education, perspectives, and personalities. And they are secure and skilled enough as team leaders to bring out all the flavors.

» *Hearty disagreement.* HPE leaders create a forum where these variations can conflict in an open and healthy way. Creating healthy conflict—and annihilating unhealthy consensus—is difficult to accomplish, but crucial for team effectiveness.

» *Mutual commitment to uncommon results.* Very few 70/30, 60/40, or even 50/50 relationships are successful. Mutual commitment requires 100/100 relationships, where both parties are "all in" on a worthy goal.

» Humility. HPE leaders know that those with the biggest titles or the most power get a lot more from their efforts when they don't act like it.

» *Deference.* There really is no limit to the amount of good a leader can do if he or she doesn't care who gets the credit.

» Servant leadership. HPE leaders use power for good. Servant leadership is not about being subservient, docile, or weak. It's about being strong enough not to have to prove it.

» *Powersharing.* Team builders are power enhancers. They don't add; they multiply. Whatever others can do, team builders find a way to magnify it. Powersharing[6] is the clearest way to maximize the power of any team or deal.

It is possible to treat others in our organizations in the same way we would treat a joint-venture or merger partner. But it will only happen with full-hearted support of this HPE principle: commit to the relationships.

Summing It Up

HPE leaders commit to relationships, and commit to making those relationships as solid and rich as possible for everyone they touch. They know that they can't win much without their partners, and without unabashed commitment to those partners (and their partners' equal commitment to them).

HPE leaders know that logic and profit aren't the only criteria for successful relationships. Being ethical and fulfilling commitments is a key part of the equation, and somehow the universe is designed to reward this.[7]

Relationships are incredibly fragile. However strong the core—or the potential core—they must be encased in the appropriate structure and packaging if they are to thrive and prosper. High-performance ethics insist that relationships be protected to release their value.

Mutual commitment to relationships, to protecting shared vision and investment no matter what it takes, is a very rich reservoir for great organizations.

7: COMMIT TO THE RELATIONSHIPS

PRINCIPLE 8

||||||||||||||||||||||||||||||||||||||||||||||||||||||||||||||||||||||||||||||||||||||||||||||||||||||||||||||||||||||||||||||||||||||||||||||||||||||||||||||||||

SPREAD THE WEALTH

If you take theirs, you'll lose yours

THERE ARE NO luggage racks on hearses.

There are no pockets in shrouds, and we can't take anything with us. We come into life with nothing and go out the same way. It's easy to forget these simple truths in the swirl of business life.

HPE leaders don't steal—obviously. But the eighth principle of high-performance ethics—spread the wealth—encases an idea that goes much deeper than a prohibition on stealing, cheating, tax evasion, or securities fraud. It urges leaders to recognize the fact that there are more important goals in life than accumulating wealth. Money surely isn't nothing, but it surely isn't everything either.[1]

What's the advantage of becoming a billionaire if it means losing yourself in the process?[2] What's the advantage of accumulating money in the bank, but gathering dust in your soul? The obvious answer is "nothing." And yet, people do it all the time. They push what's important to the side in an effort to get their hands on something that could be gone in the blink of an eye.

Of course, money is not evil, and earning it does not make you a capitalist pig. Money does provide advantages, including the freedom and ability to make a difference that those without money can't even imagine. In this sense, we should not feel guilty about having money

149

or about spending it. But HPE leaders know that it is incredibly bad judgment to trade the only things we take out of this life—our souls, characters, and our very beings—for things that others will eventually possess (or spend or enjoy or waste or use for ghastly purposes). According to this HPE principle, *it is pathetic to think that money makes a person important, valuable, or powerful.* HPE leaders know when to say "enough," when to worry more about impact than imports, and when to stop striving and start sharing.

HPE leaders spread the wealth—their own wealth and their organizations' wealth, but never other people's wealth. Too often, people and organizations demand that the government spread the wealth of others (often to them). Yet spreading other people's wealth is the very opposite of high-performance ethics. Comedian Henny Youngman liked to tell a story about the co-owner of a retail store who wanted to teach his son about values. The store owner said to his son, "Son, let's say a woman comes in and buys a hundred dollars' worth of material. After she leaves, you notice that she has given you two hundred dollars by mistake. So here's the question: Should you or should you not tell your partner about the extra hundred dollars?" HPE leaders know which wealth is theirs to spread.

HPE leaders also know that spreading the wealth is smart and savvy and beneficial all around. They do it because it appeals to our human sense of fair play and generosity and as a result, increases performance. They do it because money, like fertilizer, causes other things to grow.[3]

This principle calls HPE leaders to watch out for others. They must learn how to work with other stakeholders (like their dealers and vendors) and make them successful, and they should expect them to return the favor. HPE leaders learn how to lead "independent" people (as though there are any other kind) like contractors, dealers, or volunteers without having formal authority. And they find out that spreading the wealth outside the organization's borders is a brilliant thing to do. When we help others succeed and pool our resources strategically, we find that everyone involved gets greater returns on investment.

Spreading the Wealth Means Building Win-Win Deals

HPE leaders spread the wealth by making sure their business relationships are always win-win rather than win-lose, win-crush, or win-destroy. They know that every leader actually has to make a choice when it comes to greed, and that investing in the success of others invariably produces better results for themselves as well. The bottom line is that high performance is more than just a by-product of good ethics; it's the *direct result*.

> One Japanese executive used the term "barking dog" to describe dealers. Whenever I heard the phrase, I couldn't help but think of the many years Lanier had been a dealer, as well as the years we had spent working with dealers who sold our products. Dealers can be aggravating, but often they serve to sound a warning—a message manufacturers and suppliers need to hear.
>
> New products always have a learning curve. There are problems that have to be worked out, and dealers play a vital role in giving suppliers that feedback. They are often much more candid about product failures and features than the supplier's own people since dealers don't "report" to suppliers and are not afraid that what is said might endanger their futures.
>
> The executives at 3M referred to their dealers as the "loyal opposition." The best dealers are quick to point out problems in products, policy, and marketing plans, but they are also extremely loyal to the supplier, sometimes even refusing to take on competing products. When suppliers and dealers work for each other's success as well as their own, both profit.

Are those outsiders who work with your organization—independent contractors, suppliers, dealers, partner agencies, volunteers—"barking dogs" or "loyal opposition"? In truth, they can be both.

Our outsiders can certainly be barking dogs if we're doing something that might bring harm to them or to our organizations. And it is possible to turn some into barking dogs by the way we treat them, excluding them from the process, ignoring their input, or treating them as a necessary evil. Refusing to spread the wealth to them reduces value all around—their value to their other stakeholders, their value to us, and our value to the marketplace.

But the outsiders can also be our loyal opposition. They can tell the truth we need to hear that no one else is in a position to tell. They might say things that might miss the mark but stimulate other ideas and changes. If their opposition is prompted by a desire to maximize both their performance and ours, they're spreading their wealth to us—and we should spread our wealth to them in return. If we treasure such outsiders as part of our profitable future, we can glean every ounce of benefit from their annoying penchant to tell the truth.

Spreading the Wealth Is Aided by Courtesy

Courtesy is an important criterion for increasing the wealth for one another.

During the fifteen or more years I traveled to Japan, I had the privilege of visiting many Japanese cities and playing many of their finest golf courses. Companies like Toshiba and Sharp were great entertainers, and our Japanese hosts simply loved golf. We had some wonderful experiences and saw much of the beautiful Japanese countryside. Their courtesy and emphasis on proper treatment of customers was a wonder to behold. They were always very polite, even when things got difficult and negotiations were hard.

On one of our trips, we visited Hiroshima. We were there for the weekend, so we toured the exhibit at "ground zero," where the first of the atomic bombs that ended World War II landed. The effect of that exhibit is shocking. The older people still talk about the devastating consequence of dropping the bomb at eleven a.m. when the town was absolutely filled with workers and others. But in spite of their feelings, our hosts were always courteous to us.

After receiving such kind, courteous treatment during my trips to Japan, the first thing I usually encountered on my return to the United States was rude treatment by an airline clerk. This provided a strong contrast to the Japanese culture.

It's too easy to view courtesy and respect as weaknesses, and even as the opposite of "tough-minded management." But HPE leaders know that these values are mutually reinforcing ethics. They realize the importance of being humane and tough, courteous and guarded, respectful and skeptical—all at the same time. Bullies can win some short- and mid-term battles, but they create too many enemies along the way to be able to win in the long term.

Someone who at first glance appears to be tough-minded usually ends up being only thick-headed. It's not a very long leap from unpleasant to unprofitable. Organizations that push others around lose the extra value or business that those others could have contributed if they hadn't been pushed away. Similarly, managers who intimidate their people appear to win in the face-to-face dealings, but in the end, they lose—commitment, ideas, improvements, and ultimately the very best people.

If we aren't spreading the wealth, the only people who will stay are the ones we most need to leave.

Spreading the Wealth Is Aided by Humor

Spreading the wealth is important, but it's not always a serious business.

Once Toshiba took us to Kyushu for what they called a "green meeting," which meant we were to play golf. They took us to an old Japanese inn to spend the night. Wearing customary robes, we had dinner in a traditional Japanese restaurant that served fugu, which is blowfish prepared according to traditional

Japanese methods. A trained chef must prepare it carefully or it can be fatal. Each year in Japan at least one or two deaths result from people eating improperly prepared fugu.

As they served the fugu that evening, all of us *gygines* (foreigners) waited to see if our hosts would eat the fish. They were all grinning because they knew what we were thinking. We watched carefully as they began to eat. Then we started to eat, assuming the fugu was okay because they were eating it. As we ate, one of our Japanese colleagues smiled at us and said, "Different batch." We all had a good laugh and enjoyed our evening of cautious eating together.

One of many outstanding Japanese executives who became a good friend was Okatomi *san* of Toshiba. He spoke excellent English and had completed the Advanced Management Program, an accelerated MBA program that many executives attend at Harvard. He had a great sense of humor, as do most Japanese executives I know.

A major factor in our landed cost of goods was the strength of the dollar or the relationship of the dollar to the yen. Since we did business in Europe and other parts of the world, currency management was a major consideration, and all the Japanese suppliers shared this risk with us. I made it my practice to ask the Japanese executives what exchange rate they were using in their short-term and long-term plan. I knew that they were probably better than we were in currency forecasting.

In one of these meetings, I asked Okatomi what he thought the exchange rate would be in one year. He smiled at me and said, "Cantrell *san,* if I knew the answer to that question, that is much better business than copying machine business."

HPE leaders are generally leery about doing business with people who have no sense of humor. A lack of humor can often be an outward manifestation of a cold-blooded, money-grasping core. Working with an organization like that is like dealing with a vampire: It's deadly serious and focused, but you won't like what it does to you as the relationship evolves.

Spreading Wealth Requires a Symbiotic Relationship

The truth is, we need to get very close to our outsiders if we want to get high performance and get it in an elegantly ethical way. We have to become them, and we have to insist that they become us.

> In the late 1950s, Lanier was a dealer for 3M copiers. An aggressive, marketing-oriented company, 3M had strong field representation, unlike Gray Audograph, whose people never visited us in the field. We greatly benefited from 3M's class and professionalism. But at one conference 3M held for its dealers, Hicks Lanier showed great disdain for the 3M people—as he did for all suppliers. He instructed us not to spend time with them, and he even chartered a bus for our group so that we would not have to be with the 3M people. It was easy to figure out what Hicks was up to. He wanted to keep the 3M folks on the defensive in order to get more out of them. In addition, he knew that 3M had a history of new products that didn't work well at the outset and he didn't want us to be a part of the field research and development. In short, he wanted to wait on the new products until they were proven by actual customer use.
>
> Mr. Lanier's response was typical of most dealers. Dealers simply didn't want to invest in completing a product and getting it ready for the market. They believed this to be the job of the manufacturer. Their candor about the supplier's products could be useful if the supplier is willing to listen. Perhaps Hicks Lanier was the original "barking dog"!
>
> Since the 3M executives understood and anticipated this reaction, we heard passionate speeches from 3M executives over the years urging us to "bet with the house." And of course there

was the famous turtle award. "Behold the turtle: He only makes progress when he sticks his neck out!" It's interesting that years later, I found myself using these same speeches to *our* dealers, urging them to get started with new products before the competition got a head start. Looking back, I can see that our relationship with 3M was extremely instrumental in the growth and development of Lanier.

Suppliers and dealers have a symbiotic relationship, or at least they should. If the partnership is put into practice well, suppliers gain truth, which leads to a more ethical operation and greater volume, which leads to higher performance. Dealers get better product, prices, and market opportunity, which prevents the need to cut corners or short-change customers, which leads to ethical high performance. This same multiplication of value can happen when ethical partners of any kind work together closely and value each other's success.

The irony of business relationships is this: Smart leaders form business relationships in order to create more wealth, but too often those same leaders then act in ways that prevent that wealth from materializing. If suspicion, static, and greed are a part of our business relationships, the value of those connections diminishes significantly. Instead, HPE leaders work for even closer collaborative efforts— efforts that are deliberately planned and that can benefit both parties even more than their normal, unimproved self-interests do.

Spreading Wealth Means Sharing the Responsibility

Often, leaders cling to an idea that at first seems fair and reasonable: *It's not our job to do this for them.* "This" could be any number of things: helping out in a pinch, fixing a problem, correcting a mistake, repairing a relationship, making a call, leading an effort. "We didn't sign up for this," people protest; but the fact is, sharing responsibility is exactly what HPE leaders do.

Some time before we bought them, Nye Systems invited us to a meeting in Seattle. This was the first meeting I had attended that was conducted by one of our suppliers of dictation equipment. Nye presented several new product ideas and we provided suggestions for improvements. Bill Nye, the inventor, was a wonderful guy, but like most of our suppliers, he did not know how to put a sales organization together.

I had been working on an idea that would increase the sales of Nyematic units to the executive market. This was a difficult market to reach, but once people became users, they were usually enthusiastic and became committed to the system. The challenge for our sales reps was getting a chance to demonstrate to the executive the benefits of using the system. They found it quite difficult to just get in the door and demonstrate the benefits of the system.

My idea was to make a before-and-after film that could be shown to prospective customers. It had to be short and to the point, and it had to use emotion to put the prospect in the picture. I was sure this film would equip our sales reps to be more convincing in their sales presentations.

I presented the idea to the group and asked for funding. Every dealer present agreed to pay for at least one copy of the film and Nye Systems agreed to participate in funding the project. The name of the film was *Charlie and the Thought Copier*.

At first, our reps used small, self-contained projectors to show the product to the customers. Later, when the VCR became a standard, we made demo videos of almost every new product. *Charlie* was a forerunner of things to come, and it was very successful.

Gene Milner, who was incredibly stingy with his compliments, told my wife that she should be very proud of me. Naturally, she told me his comments, and it felt good to have a measure of his approval, even though he never spoke such compliments to me.

Why are we sometimes so reluctant to do the simple, profitable, ethical thing and ask our friends to help us? A number of factors could be involved:

> » *Arrogance.* "If this is our product, we should know more about it than anyone."
> » *Pride.* "This is ours, and no one has the right to change it."
> » *Fear.* "In order to get any useful input, we'd have to involve them too much in the inner workings of our business."
> » *Greed.* "Let's not share anything that they could use for themselves or share with other partners."

Refusing to work together and share the wealth means we end up with a smaller piece of the pie. But sharing information and responsibility for creating wealth often results in the creation of more wealth to spread.

Is involving others and spreading the wealth the *right* thing to do? Of course—it creates opportunity and the ability to make a difference for many more players. But is it the *smart* thing to do? Of course—it makes our offerings much more robust and our ability to exploit them much more vigorous.

Spreading the Wealth Is a Two-Way Street

What happens when one party in a business relationship drops the ball?

For example, when dealers feel that suppliers are not bringing enough to the table, they can use dramatic means of getting suppliers' attention.

Stenocord, one of our dictation suppliers, requested a meeting. Gene knew they were upset because our sales were down; we had other products that were cutting into Stenocord's share of Lanier's business.

Unfortunately Stenocord's portable dictating machine had many problems. Customers had returned many of these because the product failed so frequently. In order to make a statement, Gene asked the service department to bring in a hundred or more of these defective units and stack them around his desk. When the Stenocord people arrived, they were dumbfounded.

Gene had the advantage in the ensuing conversation as we talked about the defective units rather than listening to Stenocord's complaints about our sales performance.

On another day, an executive with our Canadian word-processing supplier was visiting, and he started to use a Norelco portable dictation device during our meeting. With a sly grin, Gene asked, "Could I see that?"

When this man handed the device over, Gene removed the cassette, threw the portable on the floor, and stomped it to pieces. Then he retrieved a Lanier portable from his desk and handed it to the visitor. "Now you've got a *good* dictating machine," he said. Gene hated competitors—Norelco was our leading competitor for portables—and Gene was making a dramatic issue of it, just for fun in this case. The story made the *Wall Street Journal.* Gene loved to make his point dramatically with our suppliers. Sometimes it worked.

Often, when one partner feels that the other is not bringing enough to the table, incentives are a good way to improve the situation.

3M introduced another powerful incentive for our sales force: They had regular contests, and in many cases the winning reps took a trip to some exotic location. How well I remember "Win Your Way to Wonewok." (Wonewok is 3M's lodge in the north woods of Minnesota.)

In 1962, we had our first 100-Club trip to Acapulco. I was a salesman in Augusta, and I was highly motivated to win that trip since Bernadine and I had never been out of the United States. That trip was the beginning; annual incentive trips became a company tradition for Lanier. We found that winning the annual incentive trip was a great motivator for our sales force. Most of our trips were to exotic locations—places that most of our reps would never get to on their own, like Hawaii, Monte Carlo, Acapulco, Switzerland, or Bermuda. They were able to take their spouses, which added to the need to win—or earn—the trip. Just imagine a wife saying every day, "Honey, are we going to Bermuda?" The interesting fact is that these winners earned enough money so they could easily have paid their own way—just part of the unique psychology of managing a sales force.

Many leaders use incentives for motivating sales teams, but non-salespeople can also be motivated by rewards for high performance and by a spirit of spreading the wealth. The use of incentives can be expanded beyond dealers and salespeople in order to spread the wealth in a constructive way throughout any organization.

What would happen if your organization agreed to give people 10 percent of the first year's savings on any new idea? *What?* you might be saying. *You mean if their idea saves us $100,000, you expect us to write them a check for $10,000?* But is this suggestion really crazy? Isn't it far more insane to say, "I'd rather have 100 percent of nothing than 90 percent of $100,000"? Is spreading the wealth really that painful?

Ultimately, for HPE leaders, the point isn't about incentives or motivating people. It's about spreading the wealth. HPE leaders plan to gain with everyone's willing (and perhaps even happy) contribution, because they know that widespread gain is better than selfish gain, growth is better than greed, and "we" is better than "me."

Spreading Wealth Is Aided by Personal Relationships

Eventually, spreading the wealth leads to personal relationships that aid the win-win[4] efforts even more.

Perhaps the highlight of my trips sponsored by 3M was the annual Crosby tournament at Pebble Beach, where we hobnobbed with the rich and famous as well as the top management of 3M. This trip gave us an opportunity to share our ideas with them and removed the filters between us and the folks who made the final decisions. We discovered that some of the top people actually did want to hear what we were thinking.

At the Crosby tournament, I met Al Huber, a 3M-sector executive, for the first time. He was cut from a different piece of cloth. Al is a gentle, genteel man who genuinely wanted to know what was going on in the field. It seemed that he sensed right away the tremendous potential in Lanier, and he was the one who opened the door for discussions that led to the Harris/3M joint venture.

Al and I took many trips to Wonewok and aboard the *Grace Ann*, 3M's yacht on Lake of the Woods in Canada. On these trips Al Huber and I continued to build a relationship that was very important for Lanier. Eventually, the business relationship deepened into a personal friendship, and today, even though both of us are retired, we continue to stay in touch.

In the professional world, personal friendships are often discouraged in favor of "relationship guidelines"—only marketing and sales people can talk to customers, only operations can talk to front-line workers, only purchasing can talk to vendors, only finance and accounting can talk to auditors, etc. HPE leaders cut these policy weeds back, allowing every relationship that can add or create value to develop to its full potential. They are appalled if, for example, they hear that their designers or producers don't (or can't) talk with those who are selling or using their product.

HPE leaders ask the following key questions:

> » Is there any compelling reason to limit conversations between these people or groups?

8: SPREAD THE WEALTH

> » If there is no compelling reason, are we doing everything we
>   can to put them in a position to relate, and then to maximize
>   the relationship?
> » If there is a possible reason to limit conversations, is the
>   potential increase in value worth the risk anyway?
> » If so, what steps can we take to minimize the risk and create
>   safeguards that will allow the relationship to move full speed
>   ahead?
> » How can we warn wealth-reducers (also known as turf watch-
>   dogs) against interfering with potential relationships or set-
>   ting up obstacles to open communication?

Should we value relationships or performance? Is success about who
you know or what you know? The two go together. Suppliers should
take care of dealers on the condition that they perform. HPE leaders develop relationships that *create* mutual value, not in *lieu* of that
value creation.

Spreading the Wealth Demands Results, Not Control

As leaders, we spread the wealth most effectively when we give up
the notion that we are in a higher position and thus deserve a higher
percentage. This allows us to lead without authority—one of the most
important practices of all.

> Among the many lessons learned from our dealers, the most
> meaningful was a lesson in leadership. In his many discussions
> about leadership, Gene's favorite examples were from the mili-
> tary. He had served as an officer at the end of World War II and
> was a student of military leadership.
>
> As he explained some of these concepts to me, I reminded
> him that the business world was rather different from the mili-
> tary. In the military, you have absolute authority. Those who
> disobey can be court-martialed or even shot as traitors during

war. This wouldn't be an option in business—although I am sure Gene would have loved to have that option! Gene was a superb motivator and leader in some ways, but he often relied on fear as a basic motivation. He was a textbook example of "reward-or-punishment leadership."

In my own position, I was learning an important skill, that of managing without authority. In working with dealers, you have very little, if any, authority. Threats of termination or demotion don't work because they are not on your payroll. To be successful in working with dealers it is necessary to develop a more service-oriented leadership style. It requires the pure leadership skills used with volunteers. Gene occasionally used these skills with dealers, demonstrating that he knew the approach even though it was unnatural for him.

In working with dealers, I learned that attitude was of utmost importance. If I was more concerned about their success than my own, then I was on the right track. Of course, this is true of all leadership situations. If your people are convinced that you are working to make them successful, they will follow you with enthusiasm.

Used for any length of time, control is a tool that replaces all other tools. For many young managers, control becomes the first tool of choice and then later the tool of habit for a number of reasons. First, it's a "no-brainer." It's a lot easier to bark orders, make threats, and list demands than it is to work in subtle ways through nuanced suggestions to build coalitions. Second, control feeds and soothes our egos and insecurities. And third, by its nature control eliminates other options because those who use control develop no other leadership skills, and no one trusts them if they try to use other approaches.

Fortunately, in many relationships, control is not an option. And even where it is available, it's never a good option. HPE leaders focus instead on securing agreement on the results they expect, and then free others to produce those results.

> As we worked with our dealers and our direct offices, we began to gain market share rapidly. The dealers' confidence in Lanier soared. We had a steady stream of new products and classy advertising, and our business was growing and profitable.
>
> Even with our growing relationship, our dealers could see that we were exceedingly aggressive and quick to buy out those dealers who were weak or couldn't pay us. This seemed to foster fear and insecurity. But you can't threaten or fire dealers; they can choose whether or not to do what you ask of them. Unless their performance is below contractual standards or they aren't paying their bills, your hands are essentially tied. In legal confrontations, the courts seem to favor small business. Using fear or intimidation simply doesn't work.
>
> In order to counter our dealers' concerns, I planned to speak to them at their meeting in Palm Desert, California. I put a lot of time and effort into preparing this speech because I knew it was pivotal. My relationship with these dealers would last for many years and I wanted their trust. The title of the speech was "Security in Performance."
>
> In my address, I emphasized to the dealers that all businesses have to please three groups: customers, employees, and owners. At Lanier, customers were number one on our priority list. But we also knew that without happy employees, the customers never would be satisfied. And, of course, our owners needed to receive a satisfactory return on their investment or they might as well invest in bonds. I also pointed out that dealers have a fourth party to satisfy. Since we were their major supplier, *we* had to be pleased with their performance or they might lose their contract with us.
>
> As distributors or dealers, they were our customers but

not the end users of the product. They were almost like employees, yet they were not on our payroll. They were not under our authority. They fit somewhere between customers and employees—not a bad place to be. They could enjoy the best of both worlds because of our intent to make both groups happy and satisfied.

If they had good performance based on our industry standards, they were as safe as babies in their mothers' arms. If performance was below standards, we would offer lots of help and suggestions. (If their performance did not improve, we would be looking at unpleasant alternatives.) In fact, the only difference between a Lanier direct office and a dealership was that we owned the district office and the dealer owned the dealership. In both cases, security was based on performance.

Gene was in the meeting room when I made the speech, and I pointed out that we both agreed totally on these policies, which were all related to security through performance: making quota, growth, hiring more sales reps, paying your bills on time, customer satisfaction, and the like. I mentioned building good relationships based on trust and integrity, but finished with the fact that the only basis of true security was outstanding performance. Gene grinned and nodded his agreement.

Based on the feedback I received, the speech was a big success. Many of the distributors asked for copies of the speech. In fact, years later I mentioned the talk to a dealer—I had lost my copy of the speech—and the dealer offered to send me a copy. He still had it.

This entire experience was an important part of developing the leadership skills I needed in working with independent dealers.

HPE leaders know that when control is exchanged for other management tools, better results are sure to follow. Does anyone really have the right to control other human beings anyway? Free, committed, passionate, thinking people will almost always outperform drones. And HPE leaders want no drones. They want people who perform, of course, but they know that outstanding performance is more than just delivering what is expected. They want people who *grow* jobs, not just people who *do* jobs.

Spreading Wealth Means Adding Value for Our Partners

Executives in industries like insurance often talk about "valuing agents as premier partners." But few ever actually ask their agents the important questions:

- » Are we easy to deal with?
- » Are we as concerned about your business as you are?
- » Are we doing everything we can to make your business profitable?
- » What can we do for you?

In other words, they never ask the type of questions that are essential to spreading the wealth profitably and ethically. Clients and customers also have to ask the right questions:

- » What can you do for us?
- » How can you add value for us so we can bring you more business or recommend your services or products?

By asking good questions, HPE leaders learn what they can do better and what they need to start doing (or stop doing). Other essential questions HPE leaders ask their partners include:

- » Do you agree with our purpose? Our vision? Are we going in the right direction?

» How about our mission? Are we working on the right critical success factors? Do we even know what they are?

» What do you think of our values and behaviors? Do we talk about the right things, and then do we walk the talk?

» Does our strategy make sense? Are we measuring and working on the most important drivers?

» Are we properly focused on results for you and all our stakeholders? How could we do this more?

These people have wedded themselves to your business and have a real, tangible stake in it. Why *wouldn't* you ask?

Partners that are not a full-fledged part of our organizations are not likely to offer these extras unless a forum has been established. They don't want to interfere, or they don't want to make us mad. They've got their own problems and their own businesses to run. They won't come to the party if we don't invite them, but they usually *do* want to be invited.

When we do well for our suppliers, dealers, and other partners, deliberately adding value to the relationship, there's a good chance that they will go beyond performance and spread their wealth of knowledge about service innovations or research and development.

With the help of Nicky Bolick's lab, Lanier had always been creative, building many accessories to improve the performance of our suppliers' products. We offered these items to other dealers and our suppliers, and when we landed in the supplier role, some of our dealers eventually did the same for us. For example, our dealer in Omaha made a modification to the Tele-Edisette that improved the product by making it more user-friendly and adding a function most of our customers were requesting. We called it the "Omaha Stepper," and we made it a standard part of the product offering.

We noticed that some dealers always outperformed our

direct offices. They were innovative and had grand ideas about improving the business. Rick Maxwell, our Cincinnati dealer, told me that they gave their customers a written guarantee of satisfaction, and he greatly encouraged me in the design of the Lanier Performance Promise.

Sometimes the very fact that those on the outside are not "us" makes their insights and suggestions even more valuable. They see our organizations in a way that we cannot see ourselves. They can help us focus on the things that really matter, in part because their focus is clearer than ours.

Spreading Wealth Means Helping Our Partners Produce

HPE leaders do well for others by showing them how to make the most of whatever they are doing.

The subject of product discounts and the resulting profits made by dealers seemed to cause the most difficulty in our dealer meetings. We diligently worked to show dealers how to make a good return, not only on their product sales but also on their service business.

We learned how to help our dealers by remembering our own experience as 3M dealers. In fact, when we celebrated our twenty-five-year relationship, we gave 3M a trophy with the inscription, "How About Some More Discount?" which was the phrase most often used in our long-term relationship.

We Can Take Theirs—But If We Do, We'll Lose Ours

A recent article on office theft asked, "Does everybody do it? Yes, they do: Everybody lifts supplies from the office. Anyway, stunningly, most of us do." Sixty-nine percent of respondents to a survey said that they had done this. One respondent said, "They owe me these little things."[5] In addition to the fact that this activity is wrong, it also causes one to wonder what other corners these people are willing to cut.

But the eighth principle of high-performance ethics is more than a shallow prohibition on cheating, embezzlement, and pilfering office supplies. There are a lot of ways to steal and to avoid spreading the wealth we should share:

> » Playing a win-lose game in a world where win-win-win-win (investors, customers, employees, vendors) is possible. We can try to get ours by taking theirs, but we shouldn't be surprised when others then plot to take ours.[6]
> » Stripping people of their opportunity to create wealth by annihilating their freedom, destroying their ability to make decisions, frightening them into stony (and non-innovative) silence, and limiting their ability to learn and grow.
> » Stealing others' sense of humanity and worth by degrading, disrespecting, and devaluing people until they are incapable of high performance. It's hard for people to produce wealth when they think they lack worth.
> » Taking credit for what others have thought and done, and appropriating their ideas and the rewards and recognition that accompany them.
> » Using deceit to strip people of their wealth—telling people that your organization is fine when it's not, that your future is secure when it's not, and that their stock and retirement are safe when they're not.

Wherever we are on the organizational ladder, we can be assured by this principle of at least one huge consequence: We will set the forces of the universe, visible and invisible, against us if we rob others of their wealth. We will lose the ability to build wealth, to enjoy it, and to share it. And we stand a good chance of losing the wealth we already have. It's a bad plan, and HPE leaders will not sign on to it.

8: SPREAD THE WEALTH

Spreading the Wealth Creates High Performance

Wealth and the opportunity to share in it are powerful motivators of the hard and innovative work necessary to create it.

Leaders often try a myriad of other approaches—fear, threats, humiliation, pleas, bribes, tricks, trinkets—to get people and organizations to perform at high levels. But almost nothing works as well as the opportunity to share the wealth, reap the rewards of great work, and own a piece of the pie. And others can't share the wealth if we won't.

As a wise observer has noted, "The worker is worth his (or her) hire."[7] Spreading the wealth is the right thing to do, and that right thing usually leads straight to higher performance.

When we choose to spread the wealth, we also start an engine of value. People see a counterintuitive principle at work—that by spreading the wealth everyone has more of it—and they are compelled to participate. It's an unforgettable principle, once people see it in action. It's also a magnanimous and fine way to live.

Summing It Up

HPE leaders have the potential—in a modest way—to create much out of almost nothing: markets where there were none, sales where there were no customers, products that never before existed, and services that invent a new playing field. And HPE leaders spread this wealth of innovation, causing it to grow, usually beyond imagination.

Living this HPE principle requires us to think in win-win ways—and more than ever before in win-win-win-win-win ways—to think of all of the people with whom the wealth and the growth of that wealth can be shared.

Spreading the wealth can be strongly supported by respecting all others in the relationship and their ability to make it better. It is also well aided by humor. Novelist Jane Austen "grasped, as a mere girl, that human beings and their daily behavior were a source of endless laughter."[8] In an ironic way, if we're serious about creating and spreading wealth, we will be at an advantage if we can do it wittily.

Spreading the wealth means building symbiotic relationships, relationships of mutually reinforcing attitudes and actions rather than unequal relationships of power and control. Along with that mutual advantage comes mutual responsibility. All parties to the relationship have accountability for how the whole relationship works, and not just their part. This responsibility requires that there be a two-way street, that either party dropping the ball triggers the other party to pick it up. And the success of spreading the wealth through the entire business relationship is dependent on the wise development of personal relationships.

HPE leaders understand that spreading the wealth means demanding results rather than control—that control is easy and satisfying, but terribly wrong and ineffective. They know it means deliberately adding wealth to their partners, even if they can't see an immediate return. They go beyond spreading the wealth directly to spreading it indirectly, by helping their partners to produce more wealth. And they are absolutely certain that taking wealth from others is a blueprint for losing all they've built and have.

Not taking wealth is good. And spreading it is even better.

SPEAK THE TRUTH

You can place a premium on truth
and kill the grapevine

HPE LEADERS PLACE a premium on truth.

They find it, face it, define it carefully, align with it, stick up for it, and make it paramount in all actions and interactions. It's so important to them that they expect the truth and demand it at all times,[1] and (opposite to the practice of many leaders) they penalize people for *not* sharing the truth.

HPE leaders understand that speaking the truth is the starting point for both ethical behavior and high performance, and that there is no way to have decent, healthy relationships *or* results if their foundation is riddled with myths, false perceptions, illusions, and delusions.[2] They want the leaders within their organizations to think clearly and accurately, and they know that speaking the truth is the only way to reach that goal.

Speaking the Truth Undercuts the "Grapevine"

Many leaders complain about the currents and floods of misinformation that run through their organizations, but what they don't realize is that they may be the main reason for that ancient human activity.

When leaders don't share information, or share it only on a "need-to-know" basis, they create an underground market for information—

the "grapevine," which includes such rotten bits and pieces as rumors, gossip, partial truths, slander, and backbiting, and in its full creative flower can generate whole alternate "realities." At worst, leaders accept the existence of the grapevine and try to manipulate it with planted suggestions and trial balloons. And at best—well, there really is no best.

In order to adequately deal with a grapevine, leaders must consistently and relentlessly stick up for truth. Sticking up for truth begins with a fundamental commitment to face it head-on. When people see their leaders facing the truth without flinching, they, too, gain a truth-enhancing mind-set. HPE leaders model this courage so that everyone will do the same.

> Storm clouds were gathering. The top salesman in the company deeply resented the fact that I had been appointed manager in Baton Rouge, the very office where he had been king. Daily it became more and more apparent that he couldn't handle this situation and that he was determined to do something about it.
>
> As a beginning manager, I was naive and trusting. But some of the salesmen I had recently hired confided in me, and I learned that the top salesman was having informal meetings during which he criticized everything I did and actually made jokes about me. He was tearing down the morale of the entire office in an effort to make me fail so he could get my job, the job that he thought he deserved.
>
> I knew that confrontation was absolutely essential regarding his improper conduct. When I finally had a straightforward talk with him, he seemed to receive it and promised to work closely with me in the future. Afterward, he came to my house and shed tears as we discussed the problem. My wife heard it all and we agreed that his response seemed sincere and that he was committed to change. But it was not to be. I quickly learned that his penchant for lying was still in play.
>
> At this point, I was extremely discouraged. For the only

time in my forty-six-year career, I actually interviewed for a job with another company. But although escape was tempting, I knew that the best solution for me was to solve the problems in my present position. But somehow I just couldn't bring myself to fire the top sales rep in the entire company.

HPE leaders know that one of the key components of speaking the truth is to confront an issue before it causes resentment. Wishful thinking hopes that the liar will get better and the lies will go away, but in reality, it only adds to the untruthfulness of the situation. Trying to be understanding only postpones the day of reckoning because lying will almost always get worse in the face of unwarranted "niceness."

Confronting doesn't always solve the problem—the person may not change, or may seem to change without actually changing—but at least it begins the important process of speaking the truth. When HPE leaders confront, they turn on the light and cause the darkness to recede.

Speaking Truth Includes Dealing with Those Who Don't

HPE leaders get rid of people who participate in this malicious grapevine, even when jettisoning the backbiters exacts a financial cost.

Backbiting and lying should never be tolerated, regardless of how talented an individual may be. Dealing with these behaviors requires confrontation. The objective is to change the undesired behavior. Sometimes it can be corrected, but often it cannot, and although the solution of severance is unpleasant, it's sometimes necessary.

HPE leaders get rid of angry, slander-mongering backbiters even when the decision seems to be opposed to the organization's immediate financial interests. And they do it very quickly.

In the midst of my struggles in Baton Rouge, I won an unexpected trip to 3M headquarters in St. Paul, Minnesota. It was an incentive trip offered by the Microfilm Products Division, and frankly, I didn't even know what I had done to win it. But I was grateful for the opportunity.

At the same time, winning a trip to Minnesota in the winter is a dubious honor. Many of my friends laughed when they heard about it. But 3M's Wonewok lodge was a wonderful retreat, and we were excited to spend a few days ice fishing, skeet shooting, and relaxing.

Before going to Wonewok, we had a three-day management training session at 3M, called Vision for Supervision. A number of highly trained experts, college professors, and 3M executives lectured on the definition of management, effective practices, and dealing with various management-related issues. I was like a starving, thirsty man in a desert, running toward an oasis. It was exactly what I needed!

While I was there, I made an important decision—I would have to fire the backbiting salesman. I decided that no one person, no matter how talented or productive, should be allowed to hold back the performance of the entire team. This is a fundamental truth, a principle in building any truly great organization.

The next decision I had to make was how to time his dismissal. Since he had worked diligently to sow seeds of discord, I felt that it would be important to draw attention to his termination, clearly demonstrating that I was in charge and that I had the courage of my convictions. I knew that some of our employees thought he would win out, and that I would be gone in the near future. Everyone needed to see clearly that this was not the case.

This salesman had won our annual incentive trip, of course. I decided it would be most effective to fire him immediately upon his return. When he walked into the office on Monday morning, bragging about what had happened on the trip, I asked him to step into my office. After he sat down, I explained that he was no longer employed at Lanier. He was shocked. I am sure that he thought his job was secure because of his top ranking in the company. He stormed out of the office in a huff.

The next step was to call a meeting of all employees. I could see both surprise and excitement on their faces as I explained the action I had just taken.[3] For the sales force, it was good news. We reassigned and redrew all sales territories and divided the terminated rep's territory among the other reps. There was an observable difference in attitude immediately. It was as though a breath of fresh air blew through all operations as a negative influence was removed and the respect for authority was clearly established. There was no longer any question about who was in charge.

Our business improved immediately. There was increased production—and the absence of the disgruntled salesman was hardly noticeable. Without his negative influence, it was finally possible to build a team committed to the company and to its leadership.

Although I was confident in my decision, I still wondered what Gene Milner would think about my firing the top sales rep in the entire company. The next day, I received a call from him.

I picked up the phone, anticipating the worst. But soon all doubts were erased. Gene said, "Congratulations! I always knew you had to fire that guy, but you had to make that decision totally on your own. It was a vital part of your growing-up process. Today you became a man, my boy."

Speaking the Truth Takes Determination

There are a number of reasons that leaders might want to postpone doing the right thing by getting rid of those who are untruthful:

» The right thing often seems like the hard thing, and for that reason more courage is required to do it than we normally have in store.

» The right thing requires confrontation. But the relatively brief pain of confrontation is usually minor compared with the enduring pain of the status quo.

» The right thing is sometimes costly. The costs involved in making a change or admitting the problem—offended customers, lost sales, a drop in production, lower quality—are usually minimal compared with the costs of not making the change.

» The right thing has a personal impact. Doing the right thing often leads to questions from managers up the line, disagreement from the team, and the need to find and develop a replacement, all of which take time and energy.

» The right thing creates uncertainty. It's normal to feel uncertain or insecure about how to do the right thing. But it is better to do the right thing awkwardly than to let the wrong thing continue "smoothly."

» The right thing never fits into a neat time schedule. But good leaders know that it is never the wrong time to do the right thing.

You can face any of these reasons that apply to you, and do the right thing. There is no question that dealing with liars and backbiters takes guts. But in the long run it's the only way to keep the organization's reputation alive. There is ultimately a high-performance reward for sticking with the truth.

Speaking the Truth Requires Perseverance

An old proverb warns, "Never think you've seen the last of anything."

A few days after I fired the dishonest top salesman, I received some shocking news. My boss in New Orleans had hired this very same sales rep to work in his district. He was more loyal to this disloyal sales rep than he was to me or the organization.

A week or so later when my boss was in Baton Rouge, he

asked me to rehire the disloyal rep. I thought not only of the lack of commitment and undermining behavior of this sales-man, but also the lies and misleading methods that he used with our customers. I had called on several of these customers to settle various problems caused by his behavior, and I had no desire to hire this guy back no matter how submissive he was suddenly becoming. I knew his return would not please our customers or employees.

I politely said no and made it stick.

Leaders create cultures tangled in grapevines when they refuse to tell people the truth or to take decisive action on behalf of truth. Because HPE leaders want to win fully, they would rather take criticism for standing up for truth than praise for papering it over.

HPE Leaders Listen When Others Speak the Truth

Leaders can also drive truth underground by refusing to listen when their people try to speak up for it.

By minimizing or ignoring input, these leaders deprive them-selves of truth. For their people, "telling it like it is" falls from being an inclusive, positive, organization-building activity to one that is secretive, negative, and organization-slamming. Leaders who've refused to listen in the past will not be invited to future discus-sions. This scenario results in fatal illusions at the top and inaccuracy throughout the organization, with a heavy dose of cynicism added for good measure.

It is incredible how little listening actually occurs in many orga-nizations. Some managers don't even listen when they've asked a question. Their goal is to make a point, not a connection. And many of the managers who do listen when they've asked a question still limit the potential for truth by not giving people a full forum for replying.

Peter Drucker believed listening to be the primary leadership skill. "As the first such basic competence, I would put the willingness, ability, and self-discipline to *listen*."[4] It's hard to listen, to wade through the 90 percent that we already know in order to get the 10 percent that might change our perspective. The very act of listening with openness and interest changes both the listener and the speaker.

HPE leaders get rid of dense, close-minded managers even when it seems to be opposed to the organization's immediate financial interests. And they do it quickly. They make hearing the truth a required leadership competency.

> Shortly after the formation of Harris/3M, we began to experience trouble within the company, stemming from the former 3M employees feeling oppressed. As a result, we had a union organization attempt in Chicago. The organizing unit involved the customer service representatives (CSRs) in our Chicago district, and I was afraid that it would spread to all the employees who had come from 3M.
>
> I called my friend Reg Hancock and asked for his help. Reg had worked with me previously on labor relations problems, and I had great confidence in him. He immediately went to Chicago where he met with our people and conducted interviews. He came back with a frightening report.
>
> These CSRs had many benefits when they worked for 3M. They had company-provided vans that they could use for personal use. They had company-paid health insurance. And on average, they made only two calls per day.
>
> When Lanier had taken over, everything changed, and the 3M employees weren't happy with the changes. "They take away our vans and only pay us mileage for the use of our own cars," they said. "We have to pay part of the cost of our medical insurance, and they demand that we make six calls per day." In addition, the CSRs felt that Lanier was constantly comparing

them to the Lanier technicians. The facts alone were daunting, but we also knew we had a serious leadership problem.

In every union organization attempt I was involved in, the primary problem was management. Poor leadership and communication coupled with arrogance and superiority are always an open invitation to union organizers. It was true that the 3M employees had to endure major changes. This required strong leadership coupled with compassion, and I was afraid that we didn't have that quality in many key locations in the company.

Sartain Lanier was totally opposed to unions; he wanted to run his own business without interference. But now it was important that I form my own philosophy. If I was also opposed to unions, did I have a sound reason other than control?

I realized that with a union, the employees would be reporting to two authorities, which would divide their attention. They would have the privilege of negotiating pay, benefits, and productivity standards with someone outside the company. The union officials would have no knowledge of competitive issues in the marketplace and would always demand more pay and benefits and offer less production. Which one would the employee love?[5] The answer was obvious.

Since I was concerned that this same thing might be festering all over the country, we called a meeting of all managers and service managers. We gave them strong instructions and training about how to lead through this difficult time. And we cautioned against the arrogant style of leadership, as well as against being constantly critical of 3M.

At that meeting, an idea was proposed by our general service manager, Vince Zolkosky. Although it was a terrifying idea, I had to admit that it had merit.

Vince suggested that we introduce a special hotline for all employees so that they could call me directly on an 800 number and leave a message. We would promise them a confidential response to their home address. This would give employees a way to let us know if they were under oppressive leadership, as well as a forum for sharing their ideas and opinions for improving the company. We hoped the hotline would make the employees feel better about their management during this time of transition and would smooth troubled waters. It was a good way to put the "good name" principle into effect for our employees.

After much discussion and with consternation, we adopted the "Tell It to Wes" hotline on a ninety-day trial basis. I was scared to death, but after a few weeks I was totally sold on the idea. Over the years, the hotline allowed us to quickly solve many problems that we might not have otherwise discovered until major damage was done. We were able to address drug use, sexual harassment, and policy violations. In one case, we discovered that a manager would not let his employees see the policy manual. No wonder they had questions! I responded personally to every message I received. This service continued to be offered to all employees worldwide for the remainder of my career and remains even today.

Meanwhile, in Chicago, a union election was coming up. We enlarged the bargaining unit to include sales and administrative employees and the union backed away, knowing that they couldn't win with this group of employees who were now largely enthusiastic about the company. This was a major victory.

Negative attitudes, cynicism, and victim-itis don't come from nowhere. All too often, managers treat these symptoms like the flu—they don't know how they caught it, but they hope they get better soon.

The first problem with this approach is that they've probably given this "sickness" to themselves through inept or oppressive leadership. And the second problem is that it isn't the flu—it's cancer.

Silencing Truth Speakers Makes Them Seek Allies

When people feel ignored or silenced long enough, they start looking for solutions, which can include complaining, blame shifting, covering up, and finding internal coconspirators. But they also might look for allies and defenders. In extreme cases, they'll bring in those defenders from the outside.

Unions (as well as many informal issue groups) are often alternate solutions to an unresolved problem. When people feel cut out—cut out of understanding, cut out of compassion, cut out of being heard—they seek help, often outside help. And when that happens, leaders must decide between solving the problem with truth and respect, or allowing people with their own agendas to take over.

When managers demean or treat their people unjustly rather than defending and protecting them, they're asking for outside intervention, from sources like the legal system and unions. Sad to say, many managers have needed such "reality checks" in order to see the consequences of their own bad management.

HPE leaders know that nothing "just happens." When they find that their organizations have somehow wandered into a minefield, they fight a quick battle to uncover truth and restore justice, rather than a long war to defend unethical managers and bad practices.

> The legal department informed me that an African-American employee had filed an EEOC suit after she was fired for tardiness. She claimed that white employees in her department were late to work just as often as she had been, but they were not fired.
>
> I requested an investigation of the time-clock records. We found that her allegations were correct. Although the woman who had filed the suit had frequently been tardy to work, others in her department were also tardy and received no consequences.
>
> I reinstated the employee to her position. The lawyers advised us that we should continue defending our case until

9: SPEAK THE TRUTH

we won, but I believed we had handled the situation justly, even if doing the right thing put us at a disadvantage.

Nine months later, a new manager fired the same employee for properly documented incompetence, which turned out to have been the real problem all along. The first manager, whom we had fired for his unfair behavior, had used the lily-livered excuse of tardiness so he wouldn't have to go to the trouble of documenting performance issues or confronting employees.

Had the first manager written the employee up properly with a thirty-day warning, she would have had a chance to correct her poor performance, and the company would have been spared a potentially damaging EEOC claim. As it turned out, the EEOC claim forced us to do what we should have been doing all along.

How can we avoid this sorry turn of events, which has plagued organizations in some industries—like automobiles, airlines, steel, and communications—for years? HPE leaders know they have to:

» *Give up autocracy.* No one wants to work for a dictator or monarch. Human beings are designed to be free and self-directing. When this freedom is taken from them, they will always look for someone to blame—and someone to help them take back their rights.

» *Involve people.* People don't attack something when it belongs to them. Leaving people out of the process is a solid method for producing alienation. Involving people isn't acting like the process is theirs—it's actually making it theirs.

» *Listen.* Who would look for someone else to listen to their problems if they already had someone who listens to their problems? Ideas like hotlines and open forums are effective ways that senior leaders or those leading large groups can obtain positive input as well as concerns.

» *Understand.* Someone once said, "The sweetest words in any language are, 'I understand.'" This doesn't mean you need to implement every suggestion. It only means that you recognize the source of those suggestions, sense how much they mean, and offer something (such as hope, the possibility of change, or follow-up) in return.

» *Address the real problems fast.* It's far too easy to let problems fester. We intend to get to them "someday," forgetting that someday is not a day of the week. By the time we get to it, however, the problem will be much larger, requiring much more attention, and may even have developed constituencies (people with a vested interest in magnifying the problem or elongating the solution).

HPE Leaders Proactively Seek Out Truth Speakers

HPE leaders go beyond passive listening. They proactively seek truth by going out into the field—wherever that field may be. They know that if they want to avoid fatal illusions, they've got to go after the truth like the gold that it really is.

> "There is no fertilizer like the boss's footprints." This was one of Hicks Lanier's favorite expressions because he believed so strongly that managers should be in the field making calls. That practice has continued in the company to this day. Many business leaders would simply be shocked to know exactly what's going on in their field offices. But leaders need the truth, most of which is available by observing the work in the field, visiting customers, asking the right questions, and listening.
>
> When you ask the questions, you need to ask in a way that gets to the truth, rather than a way that pushes the truth further from view. Once, my boss and I were discussing a technical project. When he told me what had been reported to him regarding the status of the project, I knew his information was incorrect.

I mentioned this to him, but he argued that the person in charge of this project had given him this report. Of course he believed it—it came directly from the project manager.

I suggested that we take the project manager to lunch and that I be allowed to ask the questions. As we were talking over lunch I simply asked a few nonthreatening questions. I deliberately did not hint at the answer I wanted or couch the question in threatening terms. My boss was surprised to find that his information was incorrect even though it came directly from the same person.

Often we can demand a certain answer by our method of questioning. If we have an intimidating style, people are afraid to speak truth that may offend us. An open, nonthreatening style always gets to truth more quickly.

It is inaccurate to say that we are placing a premium on truth if we won't take the time to go out and get it.

The truth is out there, on the floor above or below, in the field or satellite office, with employees and contractors and customers and noncustomers. If we don't know what's going on, it's because we don't *want* to know what's going on—at least not badly enough to make getting that kind of knowledge a priority.

In fact, HPE leaders know that sometimes even the most aggressive truth seeking is insufficient. They are actually willing to pay people to find and tell them the truth.

Sot Lanier had given me a great deal of good advice over the years; perhaps the most memorable had to do with advisors. Sot said that the ultimate quality of a company would be determined by the quality of advisors we selected. The advice of wise consultants, lawyers, and accounting and tax experts is more valuable than pure gold.

When you hire consultants, you're paying for the truth.

Leaders tend to think they have a handle on what's going on, but no one knows everything he or she needs to know. Some things can't be learned without an outsider's help because no organization is a perfectly safe place for people to speak the truth. When people know you are committed enough to hearing truth that you'll pay for a consultant, they tend to be more committed to you and your organization.

As a result of our ethical standards, the example set by our founders, and good advice from our counselors, Lanier never had any major problems with the SEC or the IRS. We never had any embarrassing public disclosures or lawsuits. We never overstated earnings, and we never had loans to top executives or any of the dangerous things that you read about today.

It all boils down to the fact that the CEO ultimately decides the conduct of a company. He or she should listen to advisors and creative ideas from internal and external sources, because ultimately CEOs must decide to lead the company on the basis of truth or their words will make no difference.

Finding advisors who can unravel our delusions is only part of the equation. The other part requires us to be willing—*before* we hear the advice—to act on it. We can't wait to see what the advice is before deciding to act on it. A predisposition to act is what turns the advice into pure gold.

The norm in today's organizations is to avoid outside advisors (unless their advice is required for legal or other reasons). If pushed by the board of directors, market forces, competitive position, or employee turnover, most organizations will reluctantly work their way down the following scale, sequentially bringing in advisors who:

» Make them feel comfortable and tell them what they want to hear (and probably already know)

» Tell them some new things that feel safe and don't annoy them in any way

» Tell them some new things that push them into new thinking or acting, but along the same lines

» Move them into entirely new directions in a nonprovocative way

» Provoke them into real, substantial, high-performance change in selected areas

» Cause them to reevaluate their core, keep the best of what is there, and pitch everything else no matter how long they've been thinking or doing it. This is where HPE leaders like to live.

Far too many consultants have given consulting a bad name because they do *not* place a premium on truth. They know where the safe places are, and they stay firmly ensconced in them. They charge a lot to tell leaders that what they are doing is mostly fine, to confirm what they already know, to assure them that the problem is "out there" (staff, market, etc.) rather than "in here" (leadership, cultural or organizational design, etc.), or to assure them that a serious problem can be fixed with an evolution rather than a revolution.

Is there a test for consultants and outside advisors? Absolutely. They need to measure up to five top-line criteria:

» *Wisdom.* HPE leaders don't just need people who know things. Most professionals in a field know things. They need people who know how things connect, what's important and what's secondary, and how to use their experience in a way that adds subtlety and nuance to the knowledge.

» *Understanding.* HPE leaders need people who understand people as well as their field. What they know isn't going to be helpful if they can't relate it to actual employees, customers, or other stakeholders.

» *Honesty.* HPE leaders work hard to find advisors who will tell the truth, the whole truth, and nothing but the truth, so help them God. They need to know that these advisors will tell the truth when it's pleasant, when it's unpleasant, when it hurts, because it hurts—and all because they know this is the path to higher performance and ethical behavior.

» *Affability.* HPE leaders need people who are personable, likeable, and kind enough (and sympathetic and empathetic enough) that when they tell the ugly truth, it somehow seems palatable. People sometimes need the iron fist, but they always need it encased in a velvet glove.

» *Passion.* HPE leaders need advisors who are totally committed to those leaders and to their vision, mission, values, and goals—and not just committed to selling advice. HPE leaders need advisors who want them to win.

Speaking the truth can be costly—for internal leaders and outside consultants alike. People who value truth highly dig until they find it, keep saying it until someone hears it, urge people to accept it, and push them to act on it.

Speaking the Truth Can Create Enemies

Truth-telling is a great approach for producing outstanding results, but it's also a great approach for disturbing the status quo and annoying its well-entrenched sentries. In the face of truth, those people who want to take our organizations into the wilderness of shoddy, low-performance ethics may very well react by taking aim at the truth teller.

> It had come to my attention that one of our high-ranking officers was involved in very risky behavior, so I conducted an investigation. Part of that investigation included a confrontation with the offending party and one of his direct reports. All the evidence indicated that he was guilty, and I was prepared to fire him.

I received a call from my boss, Gene Milner, and when he asked to meet with me at his home, I knew that it was something serious.

When I sat down, my boss showed me a legal pad with two handwritten pages of charges against me. Apparently, the executive I was about to fire was accusing me of misconduct. I was shocked and surprised that my boss would even consider these charges against me. It was obvious that the executive's technique was to deflect attention from his guilt to me. It's classic misdirection, a technique that often works, making people forget the original target of the investigation.

In this case, the accuser took a very effective tactic with my boss. His accusations were all based on my Christian faith, and he accused me of trying to make the company into an overtly Christian company. Most of the charges related to things that had allegedly happened on our recent incentive trip to Bermuda. Gene had not been there except for the awards banquet, so he didn't know all that happened.

In the past, Gene had talked to me about "bringing religion into the company" because he was aware of my deep convictions. He thought that I might take it too far, and had cautioned me several times. I was always aware of his concern and did my best to show deference to him and his desires. Of course, I was also determined not to violate my convictions in my personal conduct.

We sat down together and began to review the list, which were all lies or half-truths. I was reminded of the fact that a half-truth is a whole lie, and as I explained them one by one, Gene came to see what this executive had done. We terminated him as I had planned.

I learned that it is possible to hold our convictions and work in a secular environment effectively. The owners of any business want growth, profits, and customer satisfaction. If they're intelligent, they also want truth, integrity, and absolute honesty. On these points there will be universal agreement. And when you deliver on these points, they will tolerate your religious convictions, provided you are not overtly obnoxious.

The alternative to risking ourselves for the sake of truth is false peace, bad business, and no integrity.

Speaking the Truth Takes Moral Courage

What if you're following a leader who doesn't want to hear the truth? When faced with this challenge, you need to summon your courage and tell the truth anyway. The alternative—for you, for the leader, for the organization, for your stakeholders, and for the future—is even more disturbing than dealing with your fear.

> Perhaps the most precarious situation in my career arose in Gene's last few years of active leadership at Lanier. It became obvious to me (and others) that Gene was involved in a questionable activity that was threatening to our company. The issue would risk tearing down the commitment and respect we had developed with our employees. Worse yet, I worried that some employees might see Gene's example as license to do the same.
>
> My decision to address the issue forced me to answer the question, "Is this important enough to risk losing my job?" Confrontation was inevitable, and there was no way to ease into discussing the problem without Gene becoming angry and defensive. I decided I had to do it. Even though he knew that I was right, Gene also was determined to do just what he wanted to do. When I confronted him, he became terribly angry. It was perhaps the most difficult time in my relationship with Gene.
>
> As time passed, it became obvious that I had made the best decision. Gene and I worked together to resolve the situation.
>
> In all of life there are times when we must take a stand, regardless of the consequences. This was one of those times.

Speaking the Truth Creates High Performance

How does speaking the truth create high performance?

Truthful assessments—of economic conditions, demographics, political and social trends, industry direction, customers, noncustomers, people, competencies, incompetencies, products, services, value—are the foundation of successful thinking, decision making, and acting. There is no way to be effective without a fairly close alignment of your perceptions with actual reality.

And truthful assessments come from a tight, unshakable relationship with truth—appreciating it, asking for it, paying for it, seeking it, creating many safe forums for it, understanding it, and aligning with it. HPE leaders love the truth, convey to everyone around them that they love it, and push them toward loving it too. When we do this, our work loses its fuzziness and takes on a clarity of focus that nothing else can stimulate so well.

HPE leaders have this close relationship with truth, a connection that breeds high performance and ethical behavior at the same time, driving them toward reinforcing each other.

Summing It Up

As we saw earlier, the great pharmaceutical company Merck got this principle of speaking the truth wrong—both ways. When internal studies expressed concerns about the drug Vioxx, they didn't release those results and include the necessary warning labels and guidance. They *understated* the truth. And then they went the other way, pulling the product off the market with a flurry of dramatic statements, opening the company up to thousands of lawsuits and lost sales and earnings, and tarnishing their reputation—in a company that up until then had a sterling reputation. They *overstated* the truth. Neither approach relied on the simple power of this principle: Just speak the truth.

HPE leaders aren't afraid of truth. They know that any short-term pain will be more than offset by the mid- and long-term gain that comes from building on truth. They consider the grapevine an unwelcome, cancerous growth, rather than a necessary evil to be endured or tolerated. They don't put up with or manipulate the grapevine; they simply eliminate it.

And HPE leaders invite truth in, as much as they can get and as often as they can get it. They agree with the great Danish physicist Neils Bohr that "only wholeness leads to clarity." They listen more than they talk. They listen for all the pieces of truth as they work with their teams to coalesce those pieces into a whole picture that leads to right thinking and high-performance execution.

HPE leaders "boil" the system. They want to force the poisons of false perception, myth, and harmful (or fatal) illusions to the surface so they can be skimmed off and discarded. They refuse to accept the unchallenged presence of untruth and nonsense anywhere in their organizations.

HPE leaders practice and insist upon truth-telling as a top principle. They apologize if they err, either by commission or omission. And they penalize people for speaking untruth or suppressing truth— but never for telling the truth.

Speak the truth. Not a bad motto for any organization that wants to be ethical—and that wants to be great.

LIMIT YOUR DESIRES

You can find a greener pasture,
but it may be artificial turf

DESIRES CAN BE wonderful, but when they drive us toward impulsive action they can be disastrous—especially when that impulse becomes a substitute for thought, reflection, and intelligent decision making.

If we want the greater success that results from patience, we must stick it out through hard times rather than grabbing for what we want right away. In short, HPE leaders are fully aware that they have to *limit* their desires if they want to *unshackle* their success.

The idea of limiting desires—for more stuff, more profit, a better situation, a better boss, or anything else—is certainly foreign to the contemporary mind of Western capitalism, and more and more of the rest of the advancing world. But the Puritan capitalists who helped to found the United States demonstrated that capitalism coupled with voluntary limitation of greed and selfish ambition actually leads to greater long-term wealth and stability.

We will achieve much more—no matter what path we are on—when we voluntarily limit our desires. And we get more of what truly satisfies when we accept boundaries to our natural desires. Someone "is rich in proportion to the things he can afford to let alone," wrote Henry David Thoreau.

Limiting Our Desires Makes Business More Efficient

When we're dealing with a person or organization that wants the whole loaf for themselves, toiling toward a mutually workable conclusion is messy, time consuming, and emotionally draining. If we're that way with others, we'll run into more obstacles and have to fight ever harder for ever-smaller gains.

Protecting what's "ours"—what we have, what we want, what we intend to get—often means taking strong and inflexible stands and requiring intense effort to make even the slightest move. And it can mean using lawyers less effectively—as front-line players to lead the negotiation rather than as support players to clean it up.

> Hammering out an agreement with the Japanese usually only took a few days of negotiation. In some cases it might take a week or so to work out final details. In most cases we were selling the product as soon as it came out of the factory. Usually there was no contract, just a memo of understanding. The Japanese never used lawyers in their negotiations.
>
> By contrast, when we're negotiating a contract with a major U.S. company, they always sent a negotiating team to Atlanta that included one businessperson and several lawyers. Since they sent lawyers, we had our lawyers on our team as well. Negotiations went on for months.
>
> Finally during one such negotiation, I called the manager who ran that segment of the company and complained about the process. I explained to her that by the time we had a contract, the product would be obsolete. She agreed and admitted that the company's process was very cumbersome. As a result, we missed the window of opportunity and that product never contributed very much to our results.

The core problem isn't attorneys or even process. The problem is focusing so much on what we want that we have a hard time getting it.

Limiting Our Desires Doesn't Limit Our Options

The core principle of limiting desires doesn't establish one type of career path as necessarily better than another. Some spend their entire careers working their way up the ladder in one organization, while others move around frequently. It's possible to be greedy with a long stay in one organization or in shorter stays with multiple organizations. Staying in one organization might cause us to miss a bigger influence and contribution because we refuse to limit our desires for what that organization can offer—advancement, promotions, bonuses, commissions, stock options, pensions, power, notoriety, safety, and security. Moving around might cause us to miss the opportunity to make a deep, long-lasting impact because of what the "greener pasture" might offer—more money, bigger title, more perks, opportunities to command or make deals, and travel.[1]

We are not automatically more content if we stay in one organization, or more ambitious if we start our own. We can change companies, or we can stay with one company and help it change. It's the motive that makes the difference.

Tough Times Can Remind Us to Limit Our Desires

We all encounter hardship, failure, and opposition. Unfettered success is not a formula for a healthy or sane life. It feeds delusions of omnipotence when competence may not yet have been fully attained. Failure and struggle can, among other valuable things, remind us not to be arrogant or selfish, but to work instead for long-term success.

> Gene and I were flying back from Connecticut and discussing our visit with a hotshot telecommunications company. We had been there to discuss the possibility of a merger. "Wes, did you notice how arrogant that fellow was?" Gene asked, referring to the chairman of the company. I had certainly observed the behavior he was referring to, and said as much. "Reminds me of myself about two years ago," Gene said.

I knew what he was talking about. Two years previously, we had been flying high. We had the leading market share in the stand-alone word-processing market, we were very profitable, and our stock was doing quite well on the NYSE.

IBM had introduced the personal computer in 1981 and the word-processing business as we knew it rapidly began to decline. This transition was driven by technology that changed the word-processing business from stem to stern. We had been selling the No Problem typewriting system for about $12,000 per unit. Now you could buy an IBM PC with a printer and software for around $3,000. And the service contracts were 80 percent less. This had a huge impact, since we had been making most of our profit from service. In addition, customers preferred the PC because they could use a growing variety of applications software; the PC was much more than just a word processor.

It was no secret that the business model was changing radically. The new business would not even resemble the old business that had been over two-thirds of our revenue. We were in trouble, as was everyone in the word-processing business.

To make matters worse, Gene had open-heart surgery in 1981 and was out of work for several months. We had contracts with our supplier that required volume to qualify us for exclusive distribution, so we had bought inventory that was rapidly becoming obsolete in this new market. I could not imagine a more terrifying scenario. The business was changing to a lower gross-margin model and we had a lot of debt and old, expensive inventory. Although we were still doing quite well in our copier and dictation businesses, none of the old techniques we used in the past worked in the word-processing business.

It was not often I complained to Bernadine. However, one night I was particularly depressed and she asked me what the problem was. I replied, "Last year I was riding the horse but now I only get to clean out the stable!"

When we face failure—failure that might not even be entirely of our own doing—we have two options. We can attack it with arrogance and demands, sure that we will still get whatever we want because we've gotten it for a very long time. Or we can get down off our high horses and take stock of our newfound position as stable boy (or girl). When we do this, when we avoid the arrogance and potential for greed that has probably grown like a weed out of our past success, we take the first step toward renewed and greater success.

Unfettered desires focus our attention on what we're getting and drive us to extrapolate that success into the future. But extrapolations don't work, at least not forever, because markets and technology and people—and everything else—change. Keeping our desires in check keeps us realistic in our assessments, cautious in our planning, and conservative in the management of our cash and other resources.

Limiting Our Desires Means Bringing Others In

Sometimes, making our way out of failure requires inviting others into the game, even if it looks as though we'll have to give up some potential gain or control to get their help.

> One day as I walked down the hallway, Gene was coming the other way. I could see that he was very concerned about something. He stopped and asked what I thought we should do about our rapidly changing business.
>
> I had been thinking about that subject almost full-time and had a response ready for him. I thought we should sell the company, preferably to a deep-pockets technology company, so that we would have the time needed to recover. We needed to find a bridge over our troubled water. Gene agreed and we set out to find a suitable partner.
>
> There were several other word-processing companies such as NBI and CPT that were interested in us, but it struck me that they were in the same pickle we were in.

In the middle 1970s, I had contacted Harris Corp. in Florida regarding the possibility of their building a word processor. However I was unable to contact anyone who seemed to understand the idea.

In the early eighties, Harris had announced a word processor but had never brought it to market. We thought they might be a prospect because they had no sales force. Gene made the initial contact with Harris and arranged to visit with the chairman, Dr. Joseph Boyd.

Shortly after that, both Dr. Boyd and the president of Harris, Jack Hartley, came to Atlanta for further discussion. This was my first meeting with them and I had arranged for a tour of Lanier facilities. During the day, I presented Lanier's strategic plan to the Harris executives, and it was clear that they thought there was a good fit between the two companies. Harris had wanted to develop commercial products from their technology base and they needed a good sales force. They had developed a word processor and thought we could successfully bring it to market. Lanier had wanted to add a digital PBX to our product offering and Harris had such a product in development. Harris also had a strong balance sheet and Lanier needed a safe haven. We needed time to sell off old inventory and reposition our word-processing business. Harris had long wanted a marketing function and of course Lanier had such a function in place.

Soon after that meeting, Gene and Dr. Boyd started negotiations. Our board approved enthusiastically and the deal was done. When we made the announcement, Lanier employees were neutral in their reaction. We did a good job of presenting the Harris benefits: Harris was a treasure trove of technologies and was financially very strong. They had a political action committee (PAC) that both Gene and I liked very much and they were conservative in their politics, which made us a good fit in that regard. But it was hard for many to accept that we needed to go outside for help.

Sometimes the most difficult task for a leader is to ask for help. It requires insight into reality, rather than insulation from it, but it also requires setting aside our own big ideas and plans and building something different—maybe something smaller and something belonging to someone else. HPE leaders know that, however unpleasant this might be, it beats the alternative of dwindling results and possible extinction—of their careers, their organizations, and everything they have.

Limiting Our Desires during Failure Creates Persistence

For a time, failure or change feels discouraging and even depressing, as the wind is taken out of our sails. In these moments, it's easy to feel out of the loop and as if our views are no longer valued.

It's during those times that we have choices: We can stick it out and try for a "greater good" style of win, or we can start pursuing our own interests by warring over turf, acquiring protective armor, or refusing to take any professional risk.

> During this period of time in the first year of the merger, I began to question my future with the new owners. I was allowed to keep my title as president of Lanier and my board memberships with the understanding that I could not accept any other offers for board seats in the future. Harris had a very narrow view of this as compared to most companies.
>
> In the Harris meetings, I felt that I was not received as an equal. There were many snubs and sniping comments. Harris sent its staff to work with us, and they reported back to headquarters what they thought from their own perspective. At times I referred to their function as a "staff infection."
>
> I spent much time selling and convincing my boss that what we were doing was wise and offsetting reports from those who knew nothing about the business. These "informants" often used criticism in order to make themselves appear superior. To

me it seemed that an inordinate amount of time was spent on defending rather than building.

The situation was similar to one I had faced when we were developing the team management process. We had special training programs to teach people how to work together effectively as a team. The enemy of this process was largely the fact that some felt they knew more and were superior to others on the team. They acted as if they were willing to cooperate, but unless it was their team and they could call the final shot, they didn't contribute anything of lasting value.

There can come a time when our desires are good but can't be fulfilled in our current situation, and we must evaluate all of our options. But when that time comes, HPE leaders know they need to be thinking about important issues, questions of meaning, impact, and legacy, rather than mere access to more money, power, or fame.

When we desire to take accountability for doing good things for our organizations or stakeholders, and we can't get the authority or resources (or the freedom) to do this, it may be time to leave.

Limiting Desires over Time Sows the Seeds of Success

Even during difficult times, deciding to do what's best for the organization can and will grow us into solid HPE leaders with the character we need to succeed in the long term.

One day after attending a bank board meeting, I asked a fellow director, Russell Bridges, to join me for lunch. Russell was older and had experienced many difficulties and successes in his business career. He was also a deeply spiritual man.

We went down the street and enjoyed a good hamburger while I poured out my concerns to him. Russell was a good listener and took note of every detail.

Then he explained that earlier in his career, he had been

involved in a similar merger. At first he was treated as an out-sider as the new company took over. His pride in his accom-plishment made that hard to take. All this pressure caused him to consider looking for another job.

Then he reminded me that difficulties and troubles work in our lives to develop the quality of patience.[2] He suggested that I work hard, do a good job, be responsive to my new bosses, and give it some time. He also suggested that I might even learn something from this experience.

He went on to say that this was the path he had followed and that in time the acquiring company asked him to take over total management of his old company. They reached the conclusion that he could manage it better than their staff, even though they were in the same business. He believed he was just where God wanted him to be.

That day I made the decision to commit to Harris and to give this new arrangement my best shot for the next few years. I was fifty years old and could take early retirement at fifty-five. I decided five more years would be a proper commitment. I also knew that being uncertain about my future would lead to unstable or unfocused leadership. The unfocused leader can't make up his mind—he wavers back and forth in everything he does.[3] This is the death knell for any leader.

When we hit moments of "nonsuccess," anything else can look like heaven. But it's not uncommon to find that those greener pastures are really just artificial turf.

Limiting Desires Frees Us to Create High Performance

Choosing to be patient and limiting desires is, of course, no magic bullet. The situation often remains the same as it was before we made such a choice. To think, *I've changed. I'm committed to making this work; surely this situation will come around* is optimistic, but it's not realistic. No one can control what others do. They could still try to take advantage of us and our newly made commitment—in some cases, that may even be likely.

But it doesn't matter. In making the decision to limit our desires, the thing that has changed is our character. "The highest reward for man's toil," wrote John Ruskin, "is not what he gets for it, but what he becomes by it."[4]

Before, we were subservient to the situation, maybe even victimized by it. Now we're in control, because we're in control of ourselves. Good things—including higher performance—can happen when we limit our desires, not because others suddenly develop good will, but because we're now proactive rather than reactive. We know we can stay and make a difference right where we are, and we also know that we can leave and make a difference somewhere else. The choice is ours.

The only thing we can be sure of—the only thing we should never let go of—is the fact that we can and will make a difference, wherever we are. This should make us very bold indeed.

> In all of this, I had no idea how I stood with Harris top management. I was now beginning to wonder about the future and whether I would make it with Harris.
>
> I had watched the growth of our dictation business. We had developed a digital dictation system and had the leading market share in this business. The business was at approximately $100 million in revenues and very profitable. I thought that if I could own that business, we could build from there just as we had in the past.
>
> I talked with a few of my investment banking friends and advisors and was assured that we could raise the money to buy the division if Harris was agreeable. On one of my trips to headquarters, I asked for a private meeting with Jack Hartley, who was now chairman of Harris. We had enjoyed an open relationship and he was an exceptionally good boss.

When we sat down in his office, I mentioned that I was very uncertain about my future with Harris since it was such a different company. Then I said that since I was in my fifties, if I was going to make a major move, now was the time. My proposal was that the investor group and I would buy the voice products division, including all employees and facilities that supported the division. We would make it a totally separate company, and after some preparation and development would probably take it public. I asked Jack if he could support that idea.

As Jack looked at me, I'm sure he could see the concern in my eyes. His first comment was that he "believed in Wes Cantrell." This was the first reassurance I had received that he and others at Harris believed that I had something to offer. It was not that I had been told, "You'll never make it!" But there had been no indication that anyone thought I would.

Then he proceeded to brief me on plans for the future. We were in negotiations for the joint venture with 3M and if everything worked out, Gene was to be the start-up CEO. Jack said this would last for approximately one year, at which time Gene would retire again. At that time I was slated to become president and CEO of the joint venture. Perhaps we would take it public in the future but that would be determined as things progressed. This was very exciting news.

We completed the deal with 3M and I became CEO in 1987. In the early 1990s we exited the word-processing business. Word processing was now an application that ran on personal computers, and many small software-development companies were creating new inexpensive word-processing products.

Eventually Lanier Worldwide became the largest and most profitable sector of Harris. The key was the Harris/3M joint venture and the freedom to source our own copier product line and make many acquisitions, including the purchase of 3M's interest in the joint venture. We were able to move "up-segment" in the copier business (including copiers that ran at higher speeds) and greatly increase our market share, particularly with major accounts. We were also very successful with our new digital dictation systems sold to the health-care market. In addition, we had a very successful entry into the business telephone market.

Even though there was never a strategic fit, Harris gave us the freedom and capital we needed to be successful. Overall, the merger was very successful, but it was not because of strategy or synergy. It was primarily due to the commitment of the Lanier people and Harris's wisdom to let us operate as a separate company.

The most important thing I learned from the Harris experience was definitely a spiritual lesson. We will all eventually experience times when we have a new boss or a new team. It could be the result of a promotion. Or perhaps your company is sold and there is a new culture that is quite different from your experience. Perhaps some aspects of it are repugnant to you.

Or perhaps you change jobs and find it necessary to adjust to new circumstances. When you change jobs, you won't know much about the new company until you have worked there for a number of months. This can be a frustrating experience. The fact is that everyone who works will eventually face one of these circumstances. And the difficult lesson these circumstances teach us is the need for both patience and boldness.

Patience and boldness are a long way from greed and boldness. Patience pushes us to be bold because we see the good that can come from limiting our desires as well as the good that can come from receiving them. Greed pushes us to be bold because we can only see the good that can come from getting what we want.

HPE leaders are willing to limit their desires to achieve a greater good, or to try to find other avenues for those good desires that will benefit many. They know that just when things look impossible, a bigger success might be just on the other side—if they work and wait.

Good principles lead to good results. Ethics, in the full sense of that word, lead to high performance. And self-discipline about our desires—a willingness to impose limits on ourselves—is a high-performance ethic that will set an ambitious person apart from the crowd.

Summing It Up

The tenth principle—limiting desires—reminds HPE leaders to keep all-too-prevalent greed from ruining their lives.

One big problem with greed is that it is wrong. It puts "me" ahead of everything else—or worse, it puts everything else ahead of the soul. We won't have time to think about and plan and live ethical, meaningful, satisfying, contributing lives if we're too busy going after what we want right now.

But greed is also ignorant. Greener pastures are almost never as green as they look from this side of the fence. Greed offers one of the great—and often fatal—illusions of life. It promises satisfaction *if we'll only remain unsatisfied*, a dull-witted bargain that HPE leaders vet and reject.

But this principle isn't an excuse to flounder in a miserable, soul-destroying, uncorrectable situation. The push to "soldier on" in a pointless war that consumes lives is false and destructive ideology. The compulsion to "keep your shoulder to the wheel" when you're being ground to bits as a serf of an uncaring aristocracy should be replaced by a personal revolution.

As HPE leaders, we should limit our desires when those desires are wrong, when they push us to take what belongs to others. But we should also limit our desires when they are wrong for *us*—when they distract us from greater good and goals, when they steal our focus from what's really important, and when they can prevent us from actually getting those very desires.

One large component of wisdom is knowing when to say

"enough."[5] "The sense of dignity grows with the ability to say no to oneself," observed Abraham Joshua Heschel. We can't be rich if we spend all we have. Prosperity, for those who haven't been given everything from the beginning, is a by-product of passion, commitment, and good thinking—and a willingness to limit desires. "The leader who basically focuses on himself or herself is going to mislead," warns Peter Drucker.[6]

There is a big difference between limiting desires and having no desires. As HPE leaders, we should act on our desires when those desires are right, when they push us to share who we are and what we have with others. In general, the desire to *do* is better than the desire to *have*. Changing jobs to accomplish more is a better path than changing jobs to acquire more.

The desire to create is at the core of entrepreneurship and intrapreneurship, as well as better things for all. The desire to build and grow is the generator of nearly all new jobs and wealth. The desire to better ourselves—our character, which truly is destiny—is one of the main purposes of this life and makes everything richer.

And this is the paradox that HPE leaders sense and believe and learn to act upon. The way to have the desire of our hearts—for success, for prosperity, for legacy, for others, and for ourselves—is to limit those very desires.

ETHICAL LEADERSHIP FOR THE 21ST CENTURY

WHAT'S YOUR NET worth?

Take a moment and determine the answer. An accurate answer. What are you really *worth*?

As soon as you saw that question, odds are you immediately thought of your financial assets and liabilities, and the difference between them. But is a financial assessment a true measure of your net worth? Can we sum you up with a scorecard? Do you want to be remembered in terms of an accounting summary? What *will* you be remembered for?

HPE leaders—high-performance, ethical leaders—don't measure themselves that way, and they won't let others fit them into that extremely narrow box either. Their net worth is a much bigger number, tied to a much bigger concept. Components of an HPE leader's net worth include:

> » *A focus on performance.* HPE leaders understand that the only reason to have an organization at all is so that it can deliver value for others. They know that high morale is meaningless in the face of nonperformance. They orient the organization to think about results constantly and relentlessly.
> » *A determination to make performance better.* HPE leaders see clearly the difference between performance and *high*

performance. They don't measure results against what they did last year, but against what they could have done this year. They raise the bar, because anything less detracts from the organization and subtracts from its people.

» *Enhancement of the individual.* HPE leaders sense the ongoing, sustainable return that comes from a person whose passions and competencies have been released to accomplish the maximum good. They work at this directly, through dialogue, mentoring, and coaching, and indirectly, by designing an organization that values these activities. They don't accept that there are average people—they believe that ordinary people can do extraordinary things.

» *Enhancement of the team.* HPE leaders know that most teams operate below the capacity of their players. Ten people, after infighting, turf battles, and wasteful communication, might produce what five could have done alone. HPE leaders design and build teams that amplify each person's contribution and optimize the contribution of the team.

» Embedment of values. HPE leaders don't say, "There should be no conflict between ethics and performance." They believe that by intertwining ethics and performance, they will be the best in every way.

» *Resistance to comparisons.* HPE leaders know that no one ever copied his (or her) way to greatness. They benchmark competitors to hone their own offerings, not to figure out who they are or what they want to offer. And they don't borrow their ethics. They don't say, "Let's be truthful and open like that company over there," but rather, "Let's be truthful and open, period." They don't say, "At least we're not like Enron," but rather, "From Enron, we can learn the importance of speaking up when we see something wrong and being honest when we don't agree."

These are all very valuable elements of any leader's net worth, and they are incredibly worthwhile gifts to the organization and everyone that it touches. HPE leaders understand the comprehensive nature of their net worth and work hard to maximize its value.

Now we'll ask again: What is *your* net worth?

We hope it's a lot more than you first thought.

HPE Leadership Produces Fantastic Returns over Time

If you build it up, this net worth can indeed produce some wonderful career returns—even more than you could have asked for or imagined.

CONCLUSION

> It was a beautiful, balmy evening at sea. We were on a cruise ship with hundreds of top sales reps and their spouses, and we were having a great time.
>
> That night we called all of them together for a special announcement. For years I had dreamed of Lanier becoming a separate company, traded on the New York Stock Exchange, and just that day Harris, our parent company, had announced that they were spinning us off. Now I had the privilege of telling our top people. What an exciting moment!
>
> Earlier that day, I had conducted a video conference from the island nation of Martinique. All the home-office people were together for the announcement and there was great excitement and enthusiasm.
>
> The move toward this decision had started in late 1999, when I was at Harris headquarters for a meeting. The chairman requested a private meeting with me. I thought it was to discuss my forthcoming retirement, but instead he informed me of his decision to spin off Lanier as a separate company traded on the New York Stock Exchange. I was delighted to hear that he wanted me to stay on for another year or so and lead the new public company.

The key to HPE leadership is the dual, yet inseparable focus on ethics and high performance. There should be no conflict between the two. In a recent AMA/HRI Business Ethics Survey, two of the top three drivers of ethical corporate behavior were a desire to protect the brand and a desire to preserve customer trust and loyalty. Both a strong brand and customer trust are integral to sustained high performance, and both depend on ethical practice. On the other hand, "The pressure to meet unrealistic business deadlines or objectives is the factor most likely to cause people to compromise ethical standards"—a finding that clearly shows how an imbalanced focus on performance without a focus on principle impairs ethical behavior.[1]

In a recent article in *Performance Improvement* magazine, the CEO of a large health-services provider observed, "We teach employees how these qualities along with solid values and ethical behavior are necessary for success in the marketplace."[2] The authors affirmed that "shareholders want to invest in companies that have verifiable ethical standards."[3]

Many leaders are taking note. One analysis has concluded that "top corporate executives dub formal business ethics . . . 'transparency' and increasingly point to it as a 'wow factor' capable of improving business processes, employee morale, gross revenues and profit."[4]

Only a fool would promote an ethical person who has achieved nothing. And only a fool would promote a performance-oriented person who is ethically dense. It was said of one leader, "His people would follow him anywhere, but only out of a sense of morbid curiosity." People without results or values may be interesting to watch, but only as morbid curiosities.

Success Often Presents New Challenges

Moments of achievement are not the end for HPE leaders. Until we are off the stage, achievement will always bring new demands for performance and new challenges to our principles.

All of life, in one sense, is a test. We are all enrolled in the SOHK (School of Hard Knocks), a special, private school into which we gain admission at birth. Attendance is mandatory—we can't get out of class because we're smart or honest or nice or beautiful. The courses are always open and there are no limits on class size—if we want to learn things the hard way, there's a spot for us. All the classes are labs—they are longer, more complicated, and provide more chances to blow up the building. And we can depend on an unending supply of teachers—including low-performance or unethical people who will try to take us down. The tuition is high (paid in mistakes and failures), and there are no scholarships. We can't "test out" of any courses—every assignment is crucial to our development. We have to retake courses until we pass them or die—there are no rewards for "trying." And the cost goes up for each attempt. Finally, there is no grading on the curve—it doesn't matter how we're doing compared to others; it only matters how we're doing.

In this School of Hard Knocks, we are even tested by our achievements. The tests will come, even in our moments of glory.

> I had always dreamed of someday heading a public company, and once again it seemed my dreams were coming true.
>
> However, this dream was soon to turn into a nightmare. Harris's intent from the very beginning had more to do with preserving and enriching the parent company than with building two successful companies. All discussions were extremely one-sided, and we had to work very hard to convince the Harris management to give us a few breaks.
>
> It was to be what the investment bankers call a "cram down." Harris stuck us with as much debt as possible generated by the dividend we were required to pay them. We went into the deal with far too much debt, but I still thought we could make it. It became an extremely uncomfortable time for me— and I had thought I would be having the time of my life.
>
> One of the most rewarding experiences of the spin-off was

recruiting our new board of directors. I spent much time with some wonderful people and wound up with a great board. Sonny Ellis, a friend and confidant from the Oxford board, helped me immensely in this effort. On paper, we looked awfully risky to these new directors, but our reputation in the community saved the day.

As you might expect, we had great difficulty with the banks that were to loan us over $750 million. They were extremely uncomfortable with our debt as it related to total capitalization (at 82 percent), so we were unable to get the rating we had hoped for, a situation that increased our interest cost.

In addition, we were beginning to feel the bite of the change from analog products to all digital products, which reduced aftermarket (service and toner) margins. We were caught between much higher interest costs and lower margins— a difficult place for any management team.

We were there at the NYSE on the first day of trading— an exciting experience despite the disappointment we felt when our stock opened at a far lower price than we had expected. We looked just like other copier companies to the Street. The transition to digital was to be a tough experience for all of us in the copier business.

During the road trip, as I visited shareholders and met with analysts, I realized that they simply didn't like our position in the market. We had an excellent growth record and excellent returns in the past, but it was easy to see that this was a new ball game for us. The history looked good but the future raised a lot of questions.

During the final days leading up to the first day of trading, I had serious misgivings about whether we could weather the coming storm. I discussed with our legal counsel the legalities of selling the company after the spin-off. He informed me that the company was restricted from even discussing such an issue for a period of time under the law governing tax-free spin-offs. So I pushed this possible solution completely out of my mind.

HPE leaders know that even honors and successes are fraught with challenges that will try their endurance and their principles, but they are willing to press on in order to do right. They remember that "What we obtain too cheap we esteem too little; it is dearness only that gives everything its value."[5]

Challenges Often Arise All at Once

Many of the challenges come, of course, from the business situation itself. But other challenges come from other directions. All leaders are subject to attack from one or more of the following "Big Seven":

1. *Pressure* from the outside, which seems to come in waves
2. *Stress* from the inside, which causes us to internalize and magnify the outside pressure
3. *Fatigue*, a general tiredness that lowers sharpness and annihilates creativity
4. *Sickness*, which (depending on the severity) can range from a bothersome distraction to a crippling, dominating force
5. *Depression*, which can range from an off-kilter melancholy to stifling despair
6. *Loneliness* because of being at the top (of an organization, a business unit, or a team) and related frustration if there is no one who understands
7. *Anger*, so understandable at times but which (even when justified) eats people up from the inside

HPE leaders have to develop firewalls against these seven predators. Then they learn their limitations and plan or work around them. They minimize time spent with disturbing people or influences, and they know when "just a little more" is too much.

CONCLUSION

These challenges can have a cumulative effect that is greater than the sum of their parts. For example, dealing with a difficult situation at work or dealing with sickness are each highly problematic. But when you're forced to deal with them both at the same time, it can feel even more devastating.

> During the difficult days of our transition, I developed another serious problem. I had been diagnosed with prostate cancer three years previously and had controlled it with a rigid diet. Suddenly my PSA numbers shot up, signaling that the cancer was growing again. There was no doubt in my mind that it was induced by the additional stress I was under.
>
> When I was first diagnosed, I had searched the Bible for a special word from the Lord, and He had given me Job 5:25-27 (NLT): "You will have many children; your descendants will be as plentiful as grass! You will go to the grave at a ripe old age, like a sheaf of grain harvested at the proper time! We have studied life and found all this to be true. Listen to my counsel, and apply it to yourself."
>
> Since I already had seventeen grandchildren, the first verse was very easy to accept. The next sentence simply confirmed what I already knew. I was going to live as long as the Lord planned for me to live, with or without cancer. The promise was that I would live to a full age. The last part was most important of all. It confirmed that this was for my good. I knew I ought to give thanks in all things, whether or not I felt thankful. Somehow this cancer was reshaping my life and giving me a new experience that would bear fruit if I would simply give thanks and trust Him. I found that being a cancer patient opened many doors for me to speak and share my story with men's groups and other individuals who were going through the same thing.
>
> As a result of my rapidly increasing PSA, I consulted with my family and Larry Burkett, a dear friend and advisor. After

much prayer, research, and consultation with my doctors, Bernadine and I decided it was best for me to have surgery to remove my prostate.

The surgery went fine, but I had to be away from work for four weeks. This gave me time for thinking and prayer and I arrived at the decision that we must sell the company in order to preserve all that we had at Lanier.

I was particularly concerned about our leadership for the future. I was sixty-six years old and ready to retire. I decided it would be best to sell the company to a large manufacturing company in order to preserve jobs at Lanier and provide a good future for all our good people.

During times of multiple challenges, HPE leaders glean insights about themselves, their work, and their relationships that might not be on their radar screen during the good times.

Just as all of life is a test, all of life is also an opportunity—for those who see it and seize it. The times when we feel the weakest and most overwhelmed might actually be the times that are most productive.

HPE Leaders See Tough Times Through

HPE leaders know that even when they make a decision to move in a new direction, they don't just wash their hands of the old and walk away. They don't worry about parachutes, golden or otherwise, because they plan to stay with the plane until it lands. Ultimately, they don't even care who gets credit for the safe landing, as long as they get the plane where it's going safely.

Once again I consulted with our legal advisors and I learned that I had to wait two more months until the legal time requirement was fulfilled before I could sell the company. I had time to do some planning.

I hired an investment banker to assist, but I saw myself as the number-one salesman in selling the company. I was on a final mission to save the company and the jobs of our employees. We were facing the possibility of breaking our covenants with the banks and being placed on workouts. When this happens, a management team's ability to run the company ceases and the company is in the hands of others. They have no concern for employees or customers, only about collecting their money. To me, this was an agonizing possibility.

I had a list of five companies I thought would be the best candidates for the purchase of Lanier. At the appropriate time, I contacted the chairman of each company and began talks, presentations, and major sales efforts. Time was running out, and we needed a deal soon. The banks were starting to ask questions and we were having a poor quarter.

As we met with various companies, it became apparent that Ricoh was our best bet. They were large and very interested. They were impressed with our reputation for customer satisfaction and they loved our major accounts program. Over 40 percent of our revenue came from these accounts, and Ricoh wanted that clout in the marketplace. They were on a mission to be the number-one copier company in the world, and they had great products and a strong product development plan.

On my birthday, January 26, 2001, we closed the deal and announced it to our employees. Most were not very excited because they did not understand the alternatives that we faced. We did a good job of explaining, but most of our people really wanted to continue as a stand-alone company. But it has turned out to be a good deal for all of our employees as well as customers.

Lanier, a Ricoh company, has done very well. After the acquisition, Lanier earned the coveted J. D. Power Award for two consecutive years for being best in customer satisfaction. This was an incredibly good signal to all of our stakeholders that our core vision was still being implemented and that the company continued to function with the same values. In addition, the debt and profit pressures were immediately relieved, which allowed the company to focus on the proper strategic issues for the future.

In June of that same year, I officially retired. Ricoh brought in a career executive, Nori Goto, to serve as CEO, and he has done an excellent job. It gives me a great sense of pride that the company I poured so much of my life into is still doing well.

Our goal in trying times shouldn't be to try to survive, but rather to thrive and to exploit the opportunity these challenges present. HPE leaders know that the ending of their time or current role with an organization is not the end of the story.

When I decided to leave Hallmark Cards, we had been in extensive negotiations with a vendor on a very large contract. I had been the lead person in the negotiation, which would not be finished by the time I gave notice. I told my boss I would close the deal before I left and make it an outstanding one for Hallmark. He trusted me, and we surpassed his highest expectations. It didn't matter that I would be gone. It only mattered that the deal would go on after I was gone.

The way we handle our exits can extrapolate—both good and bad—far into the future, far beyond our last day in the role.

The End of One Opportunity Is the Start of the Next

Whenever we're finished with a situation, we get to choose our mindset. Is this the end? Or is this the beginning?

Although it was difficult, I knew it would be better if I made a total departure from Lanier. Doing so allowed me to focus on my new life as a retired CEO, and I had to face up to the fact that my identity was not in being a CEO. Rather, my significance was in being a committed follower of the Lord Jesus Christ. It is in Him that I find my significance and purpose for living.

I began to understand that focusing on the successes of the past is not where I wanted to spend my time. Discovering my focus and priorities for the future was most important. I found that many opportunities came my way that allowed me to use what I had learned as a CEO.

Having the freedom to spend time with my (now) twenty-two grandchildren, serve on various boards, mentor young men and women, take mission trips, speak, and teach has been most enjoyable. Retirement is not a time for men and women to devote their life to leisure. It is a time for maximum service in God's work. I have learned to think in terms of redirection rather than retirement.

Even though it was disappointing to be forced to sell the company, the results of that decision—both for Lanier and for me—have been a satisfying new start. And that is the essence of ending well.

To retire is to "leave office or employment, especially because of age . . . to cause (a person) to retire from work."[6] But mandatory retirement is a bad idea. Forcing people who are at the peak of their power, wisdom, and experience to leave office for an artificial reason, often to be replaced by people not half as good, is absurd from both logical and performance perspectives. It is ironic that many organizations allow non-performers who are not retirement age to remain and destroy value, while an arbitrary retirement age is used to destroy even more value.

Retirement itself, as a full-time life occupation, is also a bad idea. To retire is also to "withdraw; go away; retreat . . . to seek seclusion."[7] Of course there are times when we need to do that—when we're twenty-five, thirty-five, forty-five, fifty-five, sixty-five, seventy-five, eighty-five, and beyond. We all need to get away and recharge—*so we can go back and make a difference.* What's the point of recharging a battery if it isn't going to be used to power anything?

Of course there are times when we've accomplished all we can in a certain role or situation, and it's time to retire from it—when we're twenty-five, thirty-five, forty-five, fifty-five, sixty-five, seventy-five, eighty-five, and beyond. Why not retire from a mediocre situation when you're thirty-five or forty-five so you can make a huge difference someplace else? Should you stay on just because you're not "retirement age"?

We need to change our thinking on this. *Any* time a person reaches a point of diminishing returns, that person has reached retirement age. It's time to move on to a greater thing.

The truly terrific thing about systematic, repeatable retirement is that we really can "go from strength to strength."[8] We don't have to put up with a declining life and fading career. Our work is renewable because *we* are renewable. We can limp to the finish line—or we can cross it with a final sprint.

Life is a series of endings, and at each one HPE leaders want to "retire" on the highest possible note—leaving a legacy, preserving their organizations, preserving the jobs and careers of their people. But each of these retirements, each of these endings, is only temporary. Each of these endings should be the beginning of something else that has intrinsic worth. HPE leaders should want to make their final successful ending coincide with their own life ending.

We are called to finish well—not just at the end of a *job*, but at the end of a *life*.

An HPE Life Produces Sustainable Advantage

When HPE leaders keep unretiring, much more good can come their way.

> For the first time in my life, I was in the Supreme Court of the United States.
>
> Not only was I in the Supreme Court building, I was also standing in the well. As I walked up to the podium, Justice Clarence Thomas prepared to put the Horatio Alger medallion

around my neck. I was being inducted into the Horatio Alger Association of Distinguished Americans. What a thrill!

This award is reserved for those who started out with nothing, who began as disadvantaged people and achieved great success against all odds. Those of us who received the award that day felt as if we were receiving the Academy Award for business.

As I stood there, I thought back over my forty-six years in business—and the incredible odds against my being in this place, receiving this award. What a career I'd had! What a blessing! Amazing what God had orchestrated for someone who had started out at the bottom.

The words I'd heard early in my career, "It's either up or out!" and "You'll never make it," bubbled up in my memory. Those were hard words, but they accurately framed the struggle I had faced in the early part of my career.

You may be one of the many who are starting out with few or no advantages. But if you are willing to lead an ethical, high-performance life, and if you are willing to live by timeless principles and work with intensity and focus, you can accomplish far more than those who have a full array of advantages but squander them away through unprincipled or slothful behavior.

When you take your final voyage, be sure to go out on a rising tide.

In Closing: A Few Words from Wes

Poised on the brink of total failure, I had learned to trust my business to the Lord. And I had begun to understand failure as a major part of God's process for providing direction.

I had learned to get along with the most difficult and demanding bosses you can imagine—those who placed little value on my values. And I had learned that the Lord provides direction through these bosses, as He does through all the authority figures in our lives.

I had learned the value of wise counsel and the value of a true mentor, one whose interest is motivated only by seeking the best for you, with no self-interest whatsoever.

I had learned that pride is the ultimate destroyer of teamwork, and worse, that it limits our access to God's power and grace. I had seen how pride and unbridled ambition cause men and women to deceive, distort, abuse, threaten, and intimidate others to get what they want. In some cases I had seen this happen with those who claimed to be Christians, which was extremely hard to accept.

As I began to trust the Lord, His hand of direction and blessing became more and more obvious to me. I was promoted against all odds. Lanier was blessed with many great acquisitions at very low cost for no obvious business reason. Our business consistently grew faster than the industry. It was obvious that the Lord was shaping the future of Lanier, and He had allowed me to be at the helm.

This brought many new opportunities—and responsibilities. The opportunity to focus Lanier on the principle of a "good name" and to shape our values around the principles contained in the Ten Commandments was especially exciting to me. We made slow but sure changes, focusing on the customers, both internal (employees) and external (end users).

The Lord blessed us with many talented men and women, those who supported our new direction wholeheartedly. We became recognized worldwide for our dedication to customer satisfaction and received many awards. Right after my retirement, I was excited to learn that Lanier had received the J. D. Power Award for providing the best customer satisfaction. I knew that by establishing the "good name" principle, I had made some contribution to that achievement.

Awards, promotions, position, and wealth all were blessings of the Lord, but to receive the Horatio Alger Award and an honorary doctorate from Southern Polytechnic State University all within just a few months was overwhelming. What a way to retire! Surely the

Lord provides expressions of His love every day. But I knew these were special pats on the back from Him.

Nevertheless, when people ask, "What was your greatest success?" my answer is always the same. It is my family. The Lord has blessed us with four children, all married to wonderful Christian spouses, and with twenty-two *grand* grandchildren. They all continue to love and serve the Lord. This is a rare and wonderful blessing.

I hope that one day I will hear the Lord say, "Well done, good and faithful servant." But the extraordinary thing about the life of faith is that actually, He did it all!

As baseball legend Casey Stengel would say, "Amazin'!"

In Closing: A Few Words from Jim

Peter Drucker said that "Leadership is the lifting of a man's vision to higher sights, the raising of a man's performance to a higher standard, the building of a man's personality beyond its normal limitations."[9]

There are many ways to wealth, some of them dishonest, even scurrilous. But that's not the end of the story. At the end of the game, those ways are on the short end of a losing score.

The way the world works, wealth obtained through dishonorable, fraudulent, or devious means is temporary. HPE leaders get this. They come to understand that "Tainted wealth has no lasting value, but right living can save your life."[10]

Many leaders talk about the value of alignment. They usually mean alignment on strategic direction, plans, and goals—and this is crucial. Lack of alignment here can indeed kill our organizations. The earlier we get that alignment, the more outstanding the performance—often geometrically more. And the longer we wait to produce that alignment, the greater the internal chaos and the poorer the results. A 3 percent early misalignment left uncorrected will move us from being inches apart now to being miles apart down the road.

And so it is with the other alignment, alignment of principles and values and behaviors. Lack of alignment here can also kill our organizations, often more quickly and surely. The earlier we get that alignment—upon hiring, promoting, organizing, or collaborating—the more outstanding the performance.

Yes, indeed, *performance*. You might have expected me to finish that last paragraph with "the more outstanding the ethics." But the whole point is that ethical alignment *leads* to high performance. And the longer we wait to get ethical alignment, the greater the moral chaos and the poorer the results. A 3 percent misalignment in ethics now could move us from being inches apart now to being in disgrace and even prison later.

Enron has become the byword for ethical catastrophe and related performance failure. But it's easy to talk about a problem "out there." The real question is, How many of us are presiding over organizations that are growing up to be like Enron? We create the seeds of disaster when we build organizations that are truth-unfriendly, risk-unfriendly, mistake-unfriendly, and people-unfriendly. There are many warning signs of Enronism, including arrogance, controlled communication, and unfettered consensus.[11]

At the end of the day, organizational life is not an either/or situation—*either results or ethics*—but a both/and situation—*both results and ethics*. Being strong and being ethical are only opposites to small and petty minds. Philosopher Martin Buber wrote, "The way to live is to combine these two into a way of being, to integrate goodness and performance."[12]

My firm's purpose, carved out over several decades, is "Building Passionate, Thinking, High-Performance Organizations." HPE leaders need (in ourselves and our people) passion for high performance and passion for ethics. And just as much, we need thought about how to achieve high performance and how to make ethics integral to everything else.

Ultimately, we shouldn't have to talk about "ethical high

CONCLUSION

performance," as though there could be any other kind. Because in the end, all truly high performance is ethical.

And good ethics will *always* lead to high performance, in the fullest sense of that term.

AFTERWORD

In an ever-changing society and business landscape, we need something solid and real to hang on to. Something that tells us how to do things right, something that tells us how to do things well.

High-Performance Ethics points the way to that "something." It warns us that we shouldn't define *progressive* as "replacing old values that work with questionable new ones that might not." It reminds us that there are classic principles that never change. People always do well when they follow these principles, and always fail when they don't. This book is based on principles that are thousands of years old, illustrated with examples as current and cutting-edge as today's news.

Wes Cantrell and Jim Lucas aren't ivory-tower teachers or preachers. They're men who have lived real lives in the trenches. Their combined eighty years of experience—with its highs and lows, successes and failures, victories and struggles—opens a window on how to lead an ethical life that achieves great things, in part because it is ethical.

You will do well to take the message you've received in *High-Performance Ethics* and apply it to your life and career. I've seen thousands of leaders, and know from personal experience that the best of them are "believers and winners"—people who don't separate their values from their actions, people who know that ethics and high performance are two sides of the same gold coin.

—Zig Ziglar
Author and motivational teacher
Founder of Ziglar, Dallas, Texas

HIGH-PERFORMANCE ETHICS

The Source of the Core Principles

EVEN THE GREAT thinkers of the Enlightenment knew that although human reason was grand (and we would do well to give reason its due), it is not the ultimate source of value. "How can we retain our liberties," wrote U.S. philosopher, revolutionary, and President Thomas Jefferson, "when we forget that those liberties are a gift from God?"[1]

There is a Source. In writing this book, we have drawn on that Source extensively, starting with our framework. Using the almost universally and cross-culturally appreciated Ten Commandments as our foundation, we have "unshelled" those commandments to find a core principle inside each one that applies—that *powerfully* applies—to you right now.

In this appendix, we'd like to connect the dots, to show how we drew a legitimate and powerful leadership principle from each of those superb and ancient commands.

First Things Only

In the first commandment we're told, "You shall have no other gods before me."[2] In spiritual terms, of course, the Bible means God comes first. In all of life—including professional life—we're reminded that it really has to be God first.

From this commandment, we took the principle that HPE leaders should go far beyond simply ensuring that their work doesn't offend God. They also need to take pains to ensure that this work dovetails completely with their spiritual first priority. In other words, HPE leaders are absolutely certain that at every moment they're devoting their lives to the "main concern." More broadly, they should be certain that they're centering their organizations on worthy priorities and building them around achieving high visions. Not "first things *first*," as though we should have plenty of time for nonsense, but first things *only*, because life is too short to waste it on other things.

The Bible ties this commandment and work together when it says, "Work willingly at whatever you do, as though you were working for the Lord rather than for people."[3] The apostle Paul wrote, "Our purpose is to please God, not people . . . as for praise, we have never asked for it from you or anyone else."[4] The basis for good work is having a good reason to do it. The Bible claims that there's no better reason than doing it for God.

So how is it that in many of the so-called "Christian" places, these values—like working hard and with excellence—aren't always practiced? Surely working for God is on a higher plane than working for an organization or our families or our countries. But too many people don't do their work for God. They have all sorts of priorities, many of which ignore God or only give God lip service. A full, first-tier life cannot be built out of empty, second-tier priorities.

In fact, too many religious organizations have permitted and excused lousy performance because people are "doing it for God." It's a strange view of God that claims He is perfect, and then identifies Him with miserable effort and dismal results. Does intent count for more than execution? Or shouldn't intent be reflected in well-executed outcomes?

HPE leaders have learned that there are only a few things that make the difference in building a powerhouse life—professionally and otherwise. They find those things, and they don't let go.

Ditch the Distractions

The second commandment says, "You shall not make for yourself an idol in the form of anything in heaven above or on the earth beneath or in the waters below."[5]

This reminds us of several important points. First, there is only one God, and we didn't make Him. Second, any other gods are man-made. Third, those gods can be anything we can imagine and form with our own hands. And fourth, those false gods are a major-league distraction from the real God.

The principle we derived from this commandment is that life and business are loaded with distractions, most of which have a tremendous capacity to take our eye off our real work, and all of which must be ditched at all costs. One of the biggest problems is that people can think up and create the most seductive distractions, but we can't be great if we do this because we lose sight of what we need to be contributing now.

The Bible tells us that "greed . . . is idolatry,"[6] the very thing forbidden in the second commandment: "You shall not make for yourself an idol." Greed says, "We want what we want, and we want it to look as we want it to look, and we will go about getting it with whatever means are available."

To be sane is to say, "I want this because it will let me accomplish these life goals, and I will gain it through careful attention to my responsibilities and the critical success factors that will get me there." To be insane—greedy—is to say, "I want this because I want this—and then I'll want more." Greed confuses ends with means: It seeks money or power or influence as ends instead of seeking money or power or influence to make good things happen. It's a refusal to make a right choice between the things that are relatively unimportant and the things that are all-important.

The distractions in life are many, and some are even pleasant. But all of them, in the end, can become idols. When they crumble and our faith in them evaporates, our leadership will wither and our organizations will fade away.

One of the big distractions we need to avoid is looking in the wrong places for professional guidance. Many look for direction from motivational speakers or academic theorists who don't have real experience, leaders who look successful but may have just been in the right place at the right time, or board members who still want us to fight the last war.

As another example, sports provide a great source of motivational stories and simple metaphors, but it's a terrible place to turn for business examples. However difficult sports might be, business is a whole lot more complex. Sports consist of artificially constructed competitions with clearly defined time limits, boundaries, and rules. Sports are active only part of the year, have planning time between seasons, clearly identify all of the best players, don't require people to keep performing and improving in their forties and fifties, provide instant feedback, and plainly define "winning." Sports results are so short-term that emotions can trump skill deficiencies.

But what business has any of these qualities? HPE leaders use sports and similar fields for inspiration, not direction. If they simply want inspiration (or want simple inspiration), they might call a retired player or coach. If they want direction, they call someone who has played the much more involved "game" of business.

Align with Reality

The third commandment is "You shall not misuse the name of the Lord your God, for the Lord will not hold anyone guiltless who misuses his name."[7] The third commandment prohibits us from misusing God's name—to associate His name with ideas and actions He does not support. It's easy to say, "God said we should do this," when

He didn't, and to say "God didn't say we should do that," when He did. If we're saying that we represent God, we'd better do it right. The Bible calls on us to line our words and deeds up with Truth—with God and all He stands for.

The unshelled principle we saw in this commandment relates to the remarkable tendency of leaders to operate in la-la land—to work in what someone has called a "reality-distortion field"—and to support their illusions with claims, assertions, experts, and statistics, to claim that authority is on their side, and to declare good support for a bad cause. Older translations of the third commandment prohibit our taking the Lord's name "in vain." But if we aren't careful and thorough, we can reduce this commandment to a simple prohibition of cursing, when it really means so much more.

Far beyond telling us not to "curse," this commandment tells us to align with truth. It warns us that if we say, "The Bible says . . ." and it doesn't, we're treading on dangerous ground. And if we say, "The Bible doesn't say anything about . . ." and it does, the ground is no less treacherous. The Bible says that to align with God and what He says is to align with ultimate reality.

It is exceptionally easy to become misaligned with reality. It's easy to replace values that work in the real world with values that only sound like they might work. The only problem is that none of these people-pleasing, high-sounding, low-value values ultimately count. "Fearing people is a dangerous trap,"[8] we're told.

The apostle Paul saw this clearly: "See to it that no one takes you captive through hollow and deceptive philosophy, which depends on human tradition and the basic principles of this world. . . . These [rules] are all destined to perish with use, because they are based on human commands and teachings. Such regulations indeed have an *appearance* of wisdom . . . but they lack any value."[9]

HPE leaders know the value of the "intangibles." In a world of flesh *and* spirit, they know that the intangibles could mean far more for results than even the weightiest tangibles.

Find Symmetry

The Bible describes the principle of regular rest in the fourth commandment: "Remember the Sabbath day by keeping it holy."[10] This is rest with a purpose, rest with a special, set-aside, sacred sense to it.

We saw in this incredible commandment a principle all too frequently missed by leaders, the principle of taking well-designed rest. This principle is poorly represented by the concept of "work-life balance" because both our work and our rest are valuable, and need to be maximized rather than balanced. We see here the principle of whole-life symmetry. There's a time to work and a time not to work; the work will be better if we don't do it some of the time, and the non-work time will be better if we plan it and fill it with meaningful rest.

In another translation, this commandment is stated as, "Observe the Sabbath day by keeping it holy."[11] When we observe a holiday, we set it apart from all other days and plan special activities to fill it. The Bible calls this holiday a "Sabbath," and says that we should observe it. But the Bible is full of Sabbaths—every week, every seven years, every fifty years. The message is clear: Build a symmetrical life, a life where the work isn't being destroyed by having no breaks.

Some people of faith honor the seventh-day Sabbath (Saturday) and worship described in the first thirty-nine books of the Bible, while others honor a first-day Sabbath (Sunday) described in the last twenty-seven books of the Bible. Should we have a war over this? Probably not. But the message is clear either way: We need to take a regular Sabbath, regardless of which day.

How should we observe the Sabbath? If we're not careful, we could go into a check-the-box mode, where we start our days with the "God thing" (prayer, Bible study, meditation) and then comfortably assign Him to the back of the bus for the rest of the day. But honoring the Sabbath means we build our spiritual dimension into everything we do, and take pit stops so we can finish a race that matters.

Respect the Wise

The fifth commandment, "Honor your father and your mother,"[12] can be complex in practice. Still, even with pathetic parents, the commandment calls on sons and daughters to honor them—not to do what they say if what they say is wrong, not even to say that the *person* is honorable, but to respect the position of "parent" even if it's occupied by someone who seems unworthy.

The principle for HPE leaders? We have to find a way to respect and honor those in positions of authority in our lives, even if they aren't respectable or honorable. We do this because it's the right thing to do, and also because there's something we can learn or gain from them if we're watching, listening, and paying attention.

Those of us who had imperfect parents may be disappointed to notice that there are no qualifiers in the fifth commandment. We would like to see, "Honor your father and mother—if they're decent, interesting, helpful, cool, etc." But those extra comforting thoughts just aren't there.

And so it is with organizations. It would be a remarkable thing if we always fully agreed with those in positions of authority in our lives. What do we do when they are wrong or shortsighted? We listen respectfully, we discern, and then we separate the good from the bad. We consider the source by respecting them in their position, even as we might ignore—or offer a creative alternative to—what flows from that source.

Protect the Souls

The sixth commandment succinctly states, "You shall not murder."[13] It's way too easy to reduce that powerful commandment to a discussion of homicide.

We took from this commandment the principle that it's the HPE leader's responsibility—and privilege—to protect the lives of other people. This starts with doing no harm: We don't climb over them,

APPENDIX

stand on top of them, crush them underfoot, or treat them as costs or resources to be used up and then dismissed.

Don't kill people. It sounds simple—but is it?

For example, in the Bible God condemned people for burning their children as sacrifices in the fire. But the apostle James tells us that "the tongue also is a fire, a world of evil among the parts of the body. . . . It is a restless evil, full of deadly poison."[14] He's telling us that we can kill people—something in their spirits or souls—by what we say.

This commandment is, in a broader sense, an insistence that we don't take away *any* part of the life of any human being. We have no right to starve another soul in order to get something for ourselves. We have no right to advance ourselves over the broken lives of those we have "killed."

Respect and honesty should be a special domain for people of faith. Ethics are not something pulled out of a box of religion. They are pulled out of the Bible, but then they must actually be used.[15] We must live them fully to experience the benefits.

At least one of the things we discover when we unshell this great command is that we've got to protect the souls. We're expected to protect life, guarding it from all sorts of murderous thoughts, words, and actions—guarding it even from our own power.

Commit to the Relationships

The seventh commandment, "You shall not commit adultery,"[16] seems breathtakingly simple, and of course its literal meaning is simple. But at a deeper level, it actually deals with what it means to be in relationship with other human beings.

What principle can we derive from this commandment? It isn't just that we should stay away from affairs with our coworkers; that activity is forbidden directly by the commandment. But at a deeper level, what we saw in this command was the principle of commitment—great leaders make commitments and expect commitment, and they know they cannot win without the full-blown power of mutual commitment thriving in their organizations.

This commandment is about fidelity, faithfulness, authenticity, and trustworthiness in our relationships. It reminds us that commitments are designed to stick.

This is a fully developed concept in the Bible, but it is almost completely absent from much of organizational life (including from many Christian organizations, churches among them),[17] where commitments are often made and broken as easily as a soft-boiled egg.

Unshelling this command leads us to the idea that, after choosing relationships such as leader-employee, or contractor-vendor, or joint-venture partner carefully, we commit to their good. We don't spend our time trying to manipulate them or dominate them. Our partners aren't perfect (they're a lot like us), but without them we're unlikely to achieve even average performance.

HPE leaders know that one of their most important jobs is to design their organizations in such a way that very ordinary people can collaborate to do very extraordinary things, and that one of the core ideas behind that design has to be the stupendous power of mutual commitment.

Spread the Wealth

The eighth commandment is short: "You shall not steal."[18] If it belongs to someone else, keep your sticky fingers to yourself.

Again, the unshelled principle is not simply to avoid embezzling or taking office supplies—this activity is prohibited by the commandment itself. The larger principle we derived is that HPE leaders have a responsibility to "spread the wealth," first by protecting the spirit, morale, joy, careers, and livelihood of others, and second by looking for ways to enhance the total wealth (the compensation, satisfaction, and significance) of everyone in the organization and of the organization itself.

There are so many ways to steal—to rob people of dignity, self-worth, confidence, and pleasure. We'd rather have someone take our money than take our joy. To avoid the many forms of stealing, the Bible reminds us that at every point in our lives, God provides the opportunity and the capacity for success, as well as the success itself. If we take what He's allocated to others, in a sense we're robbing God.

We're told, "Better a poor man whose walk is blameless than a rich man whose ways are perverse."[19] People who think they win because they take what others have are leading what Thoreau calls "lives of quiet desperation." Although "money is the answer for everything,"[20] it isn't everything. Money is not to be pursued at any cost, because we're designed not to enjoy it if we get it badly.

Athletes, entertainers, or CEOs who make $20 million in a year have no apologies to make—if their work is honorable and done well. The money is theirs, fairly earned and owned. But if, in getting it, they had to sell stock in their souls, they have made a *very* bad bargain. If, in having it, they start clinging to it, stinginess can shrivel their souls. And if, in giving it, they trumpet their generosity, they've lost sight of their eternal return on investment (forever lost through their public self-congratulation) and the smallness of even a $1 million gift if $10 million could be given without pain.

Instead, the HPE approach has us baking bigger pies so everyone can have seconds rather than fighting over the last scrawny piece of a spoiled pie. It defines profits in the plural and includes every possible stakeholder in the sharing. It recognizes, simply, that "more for everyone" is a much better life motto than "all for me." Just as there are things worse than loneliness (like a really bad relationship), there are also things worse than having less (like pursuing money so single-mindedly that it finally has to be pried out of our cold, dead hands).

We can let bad leadership steal wealth from an organization when we design (or don't design) an unproductive culture, an ineffective strategy, a stifling structure, or a burdensome process. Ineffectiveness is the enemy of potential. Or we can take what isn't ours by using our positions ("After all, I'm heading this department") to steal the credit that rightfully belongs to someone else. But if we do, the Bible tells us that eventually, all accounts will finally balance. There is an Auditor who doesn't make mistakes. And this Auditor can't be bought.

Speak the Truth

The ninth commandment, "You shall not give false testimony against your neighbor,"[21] means placing a premium on truth. There is simply no justification for shading, altering, or obliterating the truth—or for allowing those we're leading to do so.

We saw in this commandment the principle that it's the HPE leader's job to speak the truth and expect the truth, as well as to counter untruth with truth and penalize people for annihilating the truth with gossip and rumors.

What is "false testimony"? Is it just a case of commission (putting untruths into the mix through outright lies), or does it also include omission (leaving truths out of the mix through silence)? Silence can be a powerful lie indeed.

It is a rare thing for someone to be concerned in a deep way with speaking the truth. But this commandment recognizes that the destructive power of false testimony is very great indeed. It takes on a life of its own. Mark Twain said that a lie could make it halfway around the world before the truth put on its shoes.

HPE leaders abhor falsehood. They know that, at bottom, it's one of the greatest destroyers of high-performance organizations and teams.

Limit Your Desires

"You shall not covet,"[22] the tenth commandment instructs. This takes us far beyond not stealing; it tells us not to want something too much in the first place.

Unshelling this commandment leads to the principle that real

APPENDIX

growth and success comes, in a counterintuitive way, from limiting our desires. Giving full vent to our wants somehow guarantees that we either won't get them, or that we won't enjoy them if we do get them. This isn't an argument against ambition—all accomplishment and value comes from good ambition—but it's a very strong argument against doing whatever it takes to get it all.

The tenth commandment tells us to limit our desires: Don't covet. These can be hard words when we're facing hardship, failure, and opposition, especially when somebody else seems to have it easy.

Being a decent person doesn't mean that we'll be rich, and it doesn't prevent us from getting down at times to the bare essentials of food and clothing. But whatever our position, rich or poor, we're told not to set our desire on what belongs to other people.

Although good ethics will prosper us, unethical people can also succeed or get rich. We're told that "a gracious woman gains respect, but ruthless men gain only wealth."[23] But there's a catch for people who depend on wealth without ethics: At the end, it won't make any difference. We don't want to spend our lives getting what doesn't count, gaining an abundance of what we can't keep.

Last Thoughts

The Ten Commandments are a rich vein to mine for useful life principles, and that is what we've tried to do in this book.

The principles we selected are vitally important, big-payoff principles that you can apply starting right now, without further doubt or debate or study.

You can take them. They're yours. You can do it.

And you can do it now.

ACKNOWLEDGMENTS

––

FROM WES CANTRELL

Without the encouragement of Larry Burkett, this book would most likely not have been written—at least my part of it. It was Larry who introduced me to Robert Wolgemuth, who in turn introduced me to Tyndale House, and I am grateful to both Larry and Robert—and to Janis Long Harris who recognized the potential for this book.

It has been a pleasure to coauthor this book with Jim Lucas. It's not often that two authors could work together on such a project and still be friends. Also, Laura Lucas has been a Godsend in editing and assembling our work.

My loyal wife, Bernadine, who has always encouraged me, seemed to believe I could do just about anything. My four children Jamey, Kandy, Wesley, and Juli are the products of her diligence, and I am grateful for their support. I'm also grateful for those "trouble-free" years when they were in high school and college.

The wonderful people at Lanier were a joy to work with and responded to my leadership in unbelievable ways, particularly in making customer satisfaction our purpose. There are so many great memories and stories that are not included here. The names of all those who were especially kind, responsive, and creative are too numerous to list. However, I must acknowledge my assistant for many years, Betty Atkins. She was such a blessing to my entire family and me. The best thing about Betty was that she liked everybody.

I am grateful to a long list of pastors, teachers, and leaders who taught me so much along the way. In fact, much of what I learned about biblical principles applied to business I heard first from one of these men. I list them in the order they came into my life: W. T. Chewning, A. Ben Hatfield, Mike Gilchrist, Bill Gothard, Carroll

Phillips, Charles Stanley, Bruce Wilkinson, Adrian Rogers, T. P. Johnston, and Johnny Hunt.

Of course, the first great pastor to come into my life was my own father, J. W. Cantrell. His steady example of hard work, sacrifice, and integrity was an excellent model for me to follow.

FROM JAMES R. LUCAS

A few good people.

The further you go in life, the more you value truly decent people, and the more you realize how relatively few of them there really are.

So I acknowledge you, and offer you my gratitude. Along the way, you've demonstrated that there is a better way to live, a better way to work, and that money is important but a lousy substitute for life or passion. I've seen a few of you in family, a few of you among my friends, and a few of you in business. You know who you are. I wish there were more of you.

As always, the Luman Consultants International team provided outstanding support—freeing up my time, helping with research, providing input, reviewing and critiquing drafts of the book. I want to single out one person. Laura Lucas, our editor extraordinaire, worked diligently on both the structure and content of the book. All along the way, she gave incisive commentary and useful suggestions. She displayed great character and excellence (and diplomacy) as she worked with two feisty authors over multiple edits.

This book would be much less than it is without her oversight and insight. She blends penetrating intelligence with deep sensitivity. Laura's associate, Susan Simon, ensured that the details were done right, coordinated our communication with Mr. Forbes and Mr. Ziglar and our many endorsers, and assisted the effort in a plethora of ways. Maryl Janson provided both support and encouragement along the way. To them and the rest of the Luman team, I offer a hearty "Thanks!"

I tip my hat to my coauthor, Mr. Wes Cantrell. The only thing harder than writing a book alone is writing one with someone else, but we came through the process with a strong connection and a realization of how much our thoughts were aligned and reinforced each other. His career speaks to his character. So do my many months of working with him. We wondered early on whether our combined eighty-plus years of experience would all fit into the same room (much less the same book). The answer is a resounding "Yes!"

I am exceedingly grateful to the many leaders who have invited us in to share with them and help them implement the critical concepts discussed in this book. It is encouraging to work with leaders who have a dual focus on doing right and doing well, and don't see these as conflicting notions. Their organizations can be found on our firm's Web site, www.lumanconsultants.com. I salute them. This is not a complete list of organizations with which we have worked—the few who insisted on operating on low-level principles have been omitted.

This project owes so very much to Jan Long Harris at Tyndale House Publishers. For some time, she had been encouraging me to write a leadership book for Tyndale, which would be my fifth book in that area but my first with this publisher. She then suggested the theme of this book. And finally she put Wes and me together. Many thanks to Doug Knox and Mark Taylor for making this book a priority. And my appreciation goes to the many marketing and sales people and fine booksellers who have ensured that this book got into your hands.

As always, no one knows better than an author's family what they have to put up with during the writing of a book. We are a close tight-knit, serious, funny, hard-charging lighthearted team. Noah Ben Shea said, "Family is a way of holding hands forever," and that's certainly how ours feels. Thank you for your patience, understanding, support, commentary, and humor—for the fifteenth time.

Finally, my thanks to T. B. for your inspiration and encouragement.

ABOUT THE AUTHORS

WES CANTRELL, the retired Chairman and CEO of Lanier Worldwide, Inc., began his career in 1955. Wes is known as a world-class leader and a forward-thinking expert in marketing and sales, a driving force behind Lanier's story of high performance.

Before retiring in 2001, Wes led a merger with Ricoh, a $14 billion copier manufacturer. He also successfully acquired and integrated several companies into Lanier Worldwide, Inc. During his tenure as President and CEO, Lanier saw consistent growth in revenues, from $93 million in 1977 to $1.4 billion in 2000, and the organization achieved sustained profitability in every fiscal year. Lanier Worldwide also attained excellent ratings in customer satisfaction, eventually winning the J. D. Power Award in its industry.

Through nearly five decades at Lanier, Wes built a history of personal performance and a reputation for integrity. He served in a number of positions, starting just out of college in sales and service, and ultimately leading the company, first as president and later as chairman and CEO. His experience has made him a noted authority on sales management, marketing, acquisitions and divestitures, sourcing and product development strategies, and leadership of multinational organizations.

Wes attended Southern Technical Institute, where he graduated with highest honors. In 2002, he received an honorary doctorate from Southern Polytechnic State University. He was named a member of the Horatio Alger Association of Distinguished Americans in 2001.

Currently, Wes is a member of the board of directors for Ann Taylor Stores of New York, Wells Real Estate Funds, the Fulton County Taxpayers' Association, and the Southern Polytechnic State University Foundation. Wes has also left important legacies through his previous work on the board of directors for the First Union National Bank of Atlanta, Edwards Baking of Atlanta, Oxford Industries, and AES Data of Canada.

Now at home in Atlanta with his wife, Bernadine Bigner Cantrell, Wes enjoys writing, teaching, golf, volunteer service, hunting, fishing, and projects around the home. He attends the First Baptist Church of Woodstock and is a member of the Atlanta Rotary Club. Wes also thoroughly enjoys spending time with his four children and twenty-two grandchildren.

JAMES R. (JIM) LUCAS is a recognized authority on leadership and organizational development. He is a groundbreaking author and thought leader, provocative speaker, and experienced consultant on these crucial topics.

Jim is president and CEO of Luman Consultants International Inc., an organization he founded in 1983. This consultancy is dedicated to developing passionate, thinking, high-performance leaders, people, teams, and organizations.

Recent clients are from sectors as diverse as health care, pharmaceuticals, medical devices, financial services, accounting, oil and gas, chemicals, forest and paper products, transportation, computer hardware, diversified manufacturing, consumer products, diversified business services, construction, state government, and federal government. They range from Fortune 1000 public companies and private for-profit organizations to not-for-profits and government agencies.

Jim is the author of four landmark books on leadership and organizational development, *Broaden the Vision and Narrow the Focus: Managing in a World of Paradox*; *The Passionate Organization: Igniting the Fire of Employee Commitment*; *Fatal Illusions: Shredding a Dozen Unrealities That Can Keep Your Organization from Success*; and *Balance of Power: Fueling Employee Power without Relinquishing Your Own*.

Jim has also written numerous curricula for business and leadership seminars, as well as many essays and articles.

Prior to founding Luman Consultants International Jim served in key executive positions in a number of organizations: EMCI, a high-tech design and manufacturing firm working primarily in aerospace components and orthopedic medical devices, where he served as president and CEO; Hallmark Cards, where he served as a director responsible for the completion of projects worth over a quarter of a billion dollars; Black & Veatch Consulting Engineers, where he served as manager of planning for the power and industrial division; and VF Corporation, where he was responsible for production and inventory control on its largest product line.

Jim is an award-winning senior faculty member of the American Management Association, where he served for several years as a charter member of the faculty advisory council. He has served as a professor in the School of Professional Studies at Rockhurst University.

Jim received his education in leadership, business, economics, and engineering at the University of Missouri (Columbia and Rolla). Jim is a member of the American Society for Training and Development, a senior member of the Society of Manufacturing Engineers, a member of the American Society of Engineering Management, and a registered professional engineer in Missouri and Kansas.

Jim has been honored with continuous listings in *Who's Who in America* (1999–2007), *Who's Who in the World* (1989–2007), and *Who's Who in Finance & Industry* (1989–2007).

Jim grew up in the St. Louis area and now lives in the Kansas City area. He and his wife, Pam, have four dynamic children—Laura, Peter, David, and Bethany.

For additional resources and information,
visit **www.highperformanceethics.com**

ENDNOTES

Introduction

1. High-performance ethics, both the term and the related concepts, are trademarked property of Luman Consultants International, Inc. Every time the term appears in this book, it should be read as *High-Performance Ethics*™.

2. Ecclesiastes 7:16-17.

3. HPE principles 1, 2, and 9 speak strongly to ways of thinking and acting that will help avoid this kind of catastrophe. George Eliot said, "Character is destiny."

4. Richard Boyatzis, in the foreword to the book *Moral Intelligence* (Upper Saddle River, NJ: Pearson Education, Inc., publishing as Wharton School Publishing, 2005), xxiii-xxiv. In this section, Boyatzis describes operating philosophies as "pragmatic, intellectual, and humanistic" and defines pragmatic as "a belief that usefulness determines . . . worth," intellectual as "the desire to understand . . . by constructing an image of how [things] work," and humanistic as a belief "that close, personal relationships give meaning to life" (xxiii-xxv). These definitions are rather arbitrary.

5. Ibid., xxvi-xxvii.

6. Ibid., xxvii.

7. For a discussion of the source of these solid principles, see the Epilogue on page 211.

8. Dorothy Marcic, *Managing with the Wisdom of Love: Uncovering Virtue in People and Organizations* (Hoboken, NJ: Jossey-Bass Inc., 1997), 190.

9. Stephen Covey, "Strive for Moral Authority," Business 2.0, December 2006, 89.

10. Ecclesiastes 9:10; see also Proverbs 16:3.

11. Amie Devero, "Corporate Values Stimulus for the Bottom Line," *Financial Executive*, May 2003.

12. Eric Flamholtz, "Corporate Culture and the Bottom Line," *European Management Journal*, vol. 19, no. 3, 2001, 272.

13. James R. Lucas, "Don't Become An Enron! Make Truth and Ethics Your Road to Success." Downloadable article available from Amazon.com or contact Luman Consultants International at U.S. (913) 248-1733 or clientcare@lumanconsultants.com.

14. Howard Schultz, quoted in "Starbucks CEO Applauds Staff Passion," Ridder/Tribune Business News, supplied to Knight-Ridder by The News Tribune, Tacoma, Washington, 15 June 1998.

15. Any ethics book with the number "101" in the title should probably be immediately discounted. One ethics book uses that very number, and

surrounds the raft of the Golden Rule with an ocean of anecdotes and quotes. Here's the real question: How ethical is it to charge $9.95 for 50 cents' worth of advice?

16. For a discussion of the sources from which we have derived the Ten Principles of High-Performance Ethics, see the Epilogue on page 211.

17. Norm Alster, "I Am Joe's Conscience: Employers Are Setting Up Ethics Programs to Teach Workers to Do the Right Thing. Is This the Wrong Approach?" *CFO*, March 2006, 27–28.

18. Ibid.

19. Ibid.

20. Ibid.

21. Mary Lou Quinlan, quoted in "Fast Pack 2000," *FastCompany*, Issue 32: February/March 2000, 234.

22. For more on paradoxes in leadership, see James R. Lucas, *Broaden the Vision and Narrow the Focus: Managing in a World of Paradox* (Westport, CT: Praeger/Greenwood Publishing, 2005).

Principle 1: First Things *Only*

1. For a full treatment of this important leadership paradox, see chapter 7 of James R. Lucas's book, *Broaden the Vision and Narrow the Focus: Managing in a World of Paradox* (Westport, CT: Praeger/Greenwood Publishing, 2005).

2. This is the VMVB process developed by Luman Consultants International (LCI). See note 9 (below).

3. For more information on this topic, see James R. Lucas, *The Passionate Organization: Igniting the Fire of Employee Commitment* (New York: Amacom Books, 1999).

4. James 2:18.

5. Oxford English Reference Dictionary, revised second edition, 2002, 245.

6. In his wonderful book *The Divine Conspiracy*, Dallas Willard notes that in the final analysis the only thing we take with us from this life is our character, the character we've developed by living our lives.

7. Annie Murphy Paul; Paul Sackett; Challenger, Gray & Christmas , "Testing, Testing," data contained in a table chart in Your Time—Money section, *Time*, 3 April 2006, 89.

8. At LCI, we have developed questions, evaluations, and approaches to get at these hard-to-quantify aspects. Although they are harder to measure, they are the most important things to measure, and a close approximation to reality here is more valuable than five-decimal-place accuracy on a lesser point.

9. Vision, mission, values, and behaviors should be read throughout the book as *VMVB™*, a trademark of Luman Consultants International.

10. Thomas J. Peters and Robert H. Waterman Jr., *In Search of Excellence* (New York: HarperCollins, 2004), 188.

11. Anita Sharpe, "Opposites Attract," *Wall Street Journal*, 23 May 1996, R6.

12. The financial ranking of companies was done by *Money* magazine.

Other top ten companies *Good to Great* missed include Forrest Labs (#7, a pharmaceutical company that doesn't even develop its own products), State Street (#8, a back-office processor for investment managers), and Progressive (#10, an insurance company). If you would like a free copy of the LCI study on the role of vision, mission, and values in the success of the top ten, please contact us at clientcare@lumanconsultants.com.

Principle 2: Ditch the Distractions
1. Proverbs 22:1 (KJV): "A good name is rather to be chosen than great riches, and loving favour rather than silver and gold."
2. Cognos/Palladium Group, "Making Strategy Execution a Competitive Advantage" (a study of 143 strategy management professionals).
3. Luman Consultants International has taken this to the next level with our *Passion Intelligence Quotient*™. It is an assessment that goes far beyond "satisfaction" and "engagement" to measure passion and commitment.

Principle 3: Align with Reality
1. From The Conference Board, "The 2005 Business Ethics Seminars: New Challenges, New Opportunities," July 2005.
2. Steve Liesman, Jonathan Weil, and Michael Schroeder, "Dirty Books? Accounting Debacles Spark Calls for Change," *Wall Street Journal*, 6 February 2002, A1.
3. Colossians 2:8, 22–23.
4. At Luman Consultants, we emphasize these processes in our *12-Part Mentoring*™ and *Succession Pipelining*™ programs.
5. Abraham Lincoln, http://www.brainyquote.com/quotes/authors/a/abraham_lincoln.html.
6. James R. Lucas, *Fatal Illusions: Shredding a Dozen Unrealities That Can Keep Your Organization from Success* (Boston: Quintessential Books, 2001).
7. Steve Forbes, "Deadly Prejudice," *Forbes*, 28 February 2005, 17. The quote and other details in this paragraph are all from Mr. Forbes's excellent commentary.
8. The Bible talks about people who are "deceiving and being deceived."

Principle 4: Find Symmetry
1. Oxford English Reference Dictionary, revised second edition, 2002.
2. *Whole-life symmetry*™ is the trademarked property of Luman Consultants International.
3. See 1 Timothy 3:4.
4. See Ecclesiastes 3:1-8.
5. Ecclesiastes 4:6.
6. James Michener as quoted in *48 Days to the Work You Love* by Dan Miller (Nashville: Broadman & Holmsn Publishers, 2005), 7.
7. The principle of the Christian Sabbath is described in Hebrews 4:9-11.
8. At Luman Consultants International, we work with our clients using our

PitStop Protocol™, a combination of problem-solving, learning, teambuilding, and action planning. These are restful—time to think, reflect, change, grow—but tightly planned like a race-car pit stop.

9. See Proverbs 22:9.
10. Numbers 8:25-26 (nasb).
11. Ecclesiastes 5:19-20.

Principle 5: Respect the Wise

1. At Luman Consultants International, we have developed tools for building mentoring into the organization's structure. We call these tools "*The LCI 12-Part Passionate Mentoring Program*™." As our clients have been exposed to this, some of these approaches seem familiar, some seem cutting-edge, and some completely change their perspective on how human beings can be developed by other human beings.
2. See Proverbs 27:17.
3. 1 Peter 2:18-20.

Principle 6: Protect the Souls

1. At Luman Consultants International, we have a "*Performance & Power Scale*™," with appropriate questions to get at the truth, that we and our clients use to get at where people are and how clearly they are thinking about themselves. We recommend that our clients not hire people who expect to climb the ladder before they know the ropes. We combine this with our unique "*Passion Scale*™."
2. We're told in many places in the Bible that we are to approach God boldly, and we are told in many places in the Bible that we are to tremble at the thought of approaching God at all—an interesting paradox.
3. The apostle Paul lambastes debasement. He talks about people with this mind-set having "an appearance of wisdom, with their self-imposed worship, their false humility and their harsh treatment of the body," but tells us that these things "lack any value in restraining sensual indulgence" (Colossians 2:23).
4. David Brooks, "A Man on a Gray Horse," *Atlantic Monthly*, September 2002, 24.
5. See James R. Lucas, *Balance of Power: Fueling Employee Power without Relinquishing Your Own* (Boston: Quintessential Books, 2002).
6. Ephesians 4:29.
7. Matthew 22:39.
8. Philippians 2:3.

Principle 7: Commit to the Relationships

1. E. M. Forster, *Howard's End*, http://www.online-literature.com/forster/howards_end/22/. Accessed 30 May 2006.
2. At Luman Consultants International, we work with clients to ensure also that

key employees are retained and that we are managing the "three sides of the retention triangle" (physical, mental, and emotional). Smart leaders use this process to "re-recruit" their key players.

3. See James R. Lucas, *Fatal Illusions: Shredding a Dozen Unrealities That Can Keep Your Organization from Success* (Boston: Quintessential Books, 2001). Chapter 14 covers the "Cooperation Illusion"—"Just give people a chance and they'll work together."

4. *Core excellencies*™ is the trademarked property of Luman Consultants International.

5. Please see chapter 2 of *Broaden the Vision and Narrow the Focus: Managing in a World of Paradox* (Westport, CT: Praeger/Greenwood Publishing, 2006). 6. *Powersharing*™ is the trademarked property of Luman Consultants International.

7. I once had a commitment to speak pro bono at a CEO forum where I had spoken before. My firm had just engaged with a new client who had a long conference, and they also wanted me to speak both early and late in the conference, the late date conflicting with the CEO forum. Our business development person had a logical recommendation—renege on the forum because it was pro bono, and take the paying engagement with a new client that offered the prospect of a lot of consulting business. But we ended up with a very beneficial forum, and with a new client who seemed to value us even more since we did what we said we would.

Principle 8: Spread the Wealth

1. We're told both that "The love of money is the root of all evil" (1 Timothy 6:10, kjv) and that "Money is the answer to everything" (Ecclesiastes 10:19). Apparently, we can't live very well with or without it.

2. In Mark 8:36, Jesus asks, "What good is it for a man to gain the whole world, yet forfeit his soul?" Too often, people want to teach us to think like a billionaire when they're really teaching us to think like a bozo.

3. Our nod to the Broadway musical *Hello, Dolly* for this insight.

4. As a side comment, a lot of "experts," especially outside the world of leadership and organizational development, have had quite a bit of fun ridiculing the use of terms like "win-win," but just because they are used a lot (or even used badly) doesn't mean they aren't valuable, that they aren't describing something very important that was fuzzy before. These critics miss the point that every field of study and labor has its own unique terms, some that are silly but many more that are merely laughable to people ignorant of their depth of meaning.

5. Jennifer Alsever, "The Ethics Monitor," *FastCompany*, August 2005, 27.

6. We're not talking here about offering an excellent product or service that gains market share at the expense of inferior offerings.

7. Luke 10:7.

8. Paul Johnson, *Creators* (New York: HarperCollins Publishers, 2006), 125.

Principle 9: Speak the Truth

1. For more detail on how leaders can do this badly or well, see the chapter on this important subject in James R. Lucas's book *Broaden the Vision and Narrow the Focus: Managing in a World of Paradox* (Westport, CT: Praeger/Greenwood Publishing, 2006).

2. If you want an in-depth, provocative look at this almost unaddressed subject, see James R. Lucas's groundbreaking book, *Fatal Illusions: Shredding a Dozen Unrealities That Can Keep Your Organization from Success* (Boston: Quintessential Books, 2001).

3. Given current legal realities, it is important that you have the proper professionals evaluate what you intend to say in this type of situation. We want to be truthful, so everyone will understand what just happened, but we also want to be careful, so we will provide no "cheap" reason for a defamation lawsuit. Because of fear, many leaders take the easy way out and say nothing, leaving the organization to its own interpretations, which are frequently faulty and can enlarge the grapevine while shrinking morale. The law is never a good enough excuse to avoid the truth.

4. Peter F. Drucker, *The Daily Drucker* (New York: HarperCollins, 2004), 113.

5. Matthew 6:24 states, "No one can serve two masters."

Principle 10: Limit Your Desires

1. Wes and Jim have taken very different paths to get where they are. Wes spent forty-six years with one organization, learning through thick and thin and seeing the business grow and prosper. Jim spent a number of years with several large and several small organizations before founding his own company in 1983, a cutting-edge consulting practice that has worked with many more organizations. Wes had tough years as he worked his way through his company, and Jim's team had lean years as they worked to build a company from scratch. The real thing we have learned is that neither course is "best" in any absolute sense.

2. Romans 5:3.

3. James 1:5.

4. John Ruskin, as quoted in *Forbes*, 24 May 1982, 192.

5. See Ecclesiastes 4:5-6.

6. Peter F. Drucker, *The Daily Drucker* (New York: HarperCollins, 2004), 108.

Conclusion

1. American Management Association, "The State of Corporate Ethics, 2005—2015," *Executive Matters*, January 2006, 1.

2. Diane Kubal, Michael Baker, and Kendra Coleman, "Doing the Right Thing: How Today's Leading Companies Are Becoming More Ethical," *Performance Improvement*, vol. 45, no. 3, 6–7. A *Wall Street Journal* article, "Managing by the (Good) Book," noted that religious principles are welcome: "Lawyers say it's generally not a problem to run a public company on faith-based

principles, as long as the executives make these principles clear to share-holders." *WSJ*, 9 October 2006, B1.

3. Ibid.

4. "Accounting for Ethics Adds Up to KC Edge," *Ingrams*, July 2006, 30.

5. English philosopher Thomas Paine, quoted in *Forbes*, 26 April 1982, "Quotes."

6. Oxford English Reference Dictionary, revised second edition, 2002.

7. Ibid.

8. See Psalm 84:5-7.

9. Peter F. Drucker, *The Daily Drucker* (New York: HarperCollins, 2004), 108. We would only change this by adding "or woman's."

10. Proverbs 10:2 (NLT).

11. James R. Lucas, "Don't Become An Enron! Make Truth and Ethics Your Road to Success." Downloadable article available from Amazon.com or contact Luman Consultants International at U.S. (913) 248-1733, clientcare@lumanconsultants.com, or http://www.lumanconsultants.com. We give detail on the four "unfriendlies," discuss the eight warning signs of Enronism, and give you eight steps to take to avoid Enronism.

12. As quoted in "God and Mammon at Harvard," *FastCompany*, May 2005, 81.

Appendix

1. Thomas Jefferson, as inscribed on the Thomas Jefferson Memorial, Washington, D.C.

2. Exodus 20:3.

3. Colossians 3:23 (NLT).

4. 1 Thessalonians 2:4b, 6 (NLT).

5. Exodus 20:4.

6. Colossians 3:5.

7. Deuteronomy 5:11.

8. Proverbs 29:25 (NLT).

9. Colossians 2:8, 22-23 emphasis added.

10. Exodus 20:8.

11. Deuteronomy 5:12.

12. Exodus 20:12.

13. Exodus 20:13.

14. James 3:6, 8.

15. Although I have worked mainly with secular organizations, four of the five significant cases in which people in business have dealt with me dishonestly have involved people who claimed to be Christians—and two of those times involved organizations that claimed to be "Christian." One company declared bankruptcy to protect the owners even though they owed me and dozens of others substantial royalties that were never paid, even in professional support (and ironically, they had the strongest "morals" clause I've ever seen in a contract). Another violated the

contract and then would not return my intellectual property without
a payment.
16. Exodus 20:14.
17. See Romans 12 for a discussion of how all the members of a team contribute
to its success.
18. Exodus 20:15.
19. Proverbs 28:6.
20. Ecclesiastes 10:19.
21. Exodus 20:16.
22. Exodus 20:17.
23. Proverbs 11:16 (NLT).

Online Discussion *guide*

TAKE *your* TYNDALE READING EXPERIENCE *to the* NEXT LEVEL

A FREE discussion guide for this book is available at bookclubhub.net, perfect for sparking conversations in your book group or for digging deeper into the text on your own.

www.bookclubhub.net

You'll also find free discussion guides for other Tyndale books, e-newsletters, e-mail devotionals, virtual book tours, and more!

Also by James R. Lucas

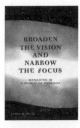

Broaden the Vision and Narrow the Focus: Managing in a World of Paradox

"One of the best business books I've read in years! Wisdom leaps off [the] page. I can't imagine anyone in the world of business not benefiting tremendously from its wealth of practical insights. . . . Open this book and meet a great teacher you'll be very glad to know!"

—**Tom Morris**, author of *True Success, The Art of Achievement*, and *If Aristotle Ran General Motors*

The Passionate Organization: Igniting the Fire of Employee Commitment

"A brilliant compendium of trenchant observations about the release of human spirit. The ultimate weapon for the 21st century."

—**Arthur D. Wainwright**, Chairman & CEO
Wainwright Industries (Winners of the Baldrige Award)

Balance of Power: Fueling Employee Power without Relinquishing Your Own

"An uncommon balance of cutting-edge management strategies and proven, age-old leadership techniques. . . . Lucas offers creative solutions to satisfy the changing management challenges of the millennium."

—**John G. Hughes Jr.**, President, Creative Leadership Strategies

Fatal Illusions: Shredding a Dozen Unrealities That Can Keep Your Organization from Success

"Lucas puts the choices right out there: We can try to live a life built on illusion, or we can go after what we really need–truth. Read *Fatal Illusions* for its sobering account of the delusions that often trap us, but even more for its guidance on how to stop 'illuding' and start living with reality."

—**Lee G. Bolman, PhD**, Marion Bloch Professor of Leadership
Bloch School of Business and Public Administration
University of Missouri-Kansas City

For more information about Mr. Lucas's career as an internationally renowned speaker on leadership, culture, and organizations, visit www.jamesrlucas.com. Mr. Lucas is also president and CEO of a provocative, thought-leadership consulting practice, which can be found at www.lumanconsultants.com. To contact the author directly, e-mail jlucas@lumanconsultants.com.

CP0086